A DREAM OF FREEDOM

A DREAM OF FREEDOM

THE CIVIL RIGHTS MOVEMENT FROM 1954 TO 1968

DIANE McWHORTER

FOREWORD BY REVEREND FRED SHUTTLESWORTH

SCHOLASTIC NONFICTION

To my daughters, Lucy and Isabel —D.M.

Library of Congress Cataloging-in-Publication Data is available.
ISBN-13: 978-0-439-57678-9
ISBN-10: 0-439-57678-4
Printed in Singapore 46 • First printing, October 2004
12 11 10 9 8 7 6   10 11 12/0

CONTENTS

WHAT ONE MUST DO

Reverend Fred Shuttlesworth

Co-founder, Southern Christian Leadership Conference

Reverend Fred Shuttlesworth

[6]

When I heard the thunderous explosion, I knew exactly what it was: a bomb with my name on it. It was Christmas night of 1956, and I was the pastor of the Bethel Baptist church in Birmingham, Alabama. The local black citizens had endured so much of the Ku Klux Klan's dynamite that our city was known as "Bombingham." But this was my first (though not my last) bomb. It had gone off right next to the bed I was lying in. The wall behind my head shattered, and the ceiling caved in around me. For some reason, a happy, peaceful feeling came over me. The 27th Psalm kept running through my head: "The Lord is my light and my salvation; whom shall I fear?"

My house, which adjoined the church, was nearly demolished, but I walked out of the wreckage without a hair on my head disturbed. My wife and children were also unmarked. There was a burly policeman outside to greet me. With tears in his eyes, he said, "Reverend, I'm so sorry. I know these people." (He meant the bombers.) "I did not think they would go

this far. Reverend, I'll tell you what I'd do if I were you. I'd get out of town as quick as I could."

I was still trying to get over my shock at seeing a policeman cry, but I replied, "Well, officer, you're not me. Go back and tell your Klan brothers that if the Lord could save me through this, I am here for the duration. The war is just beginning."

Why had the Klan decided to bomb me? You will read all about it in *A Dream of Freedom*. The black citizens of Montgomery, 90 miles to the south of Birmingham, had just triumphantly completed a year-long boycott of the city buses, to protest the segregation laws that required them to sit in the back of those buses. I had gone to the first mass meeting of the history-changing Montgomery bus boycott and had become a fellow freedom fighter of the young minister who had been thrust into the protest's leadership: Dr. Martin Luther King Jr. The Klan decided to let me know with dynamite that they didn't care for my own noisy role in the civil rights struggle. And that was where I was blown into history.

After God erased my name off that bomb, I had no fear at all about fighting for the rights of my people. I was not only bombed, I was also mobbed and jailed and sued. It was often a lonely struggle as well as a dangerous one. Then, finally came the "Year of Birmingham," 1963. The traumatic events in my hometown put the freedom movement front and center in the consciousness of America and the world. In the pivotal battle of the civil rights revolution, right there in my backyard, Martin and I tore down the walls of what I called Fortress Segregation.

You will learn about that and the other spectacular confrontations of the era in *A Dream of Freedom*. Because the conflict itself is so dramatic, I feel that I must take the opportunity here to stress what is often lost in the retelling of the civil rights struggle. And that is the faith and determination of ordinary folks caught up in a national moral crisis. During the Birmingham campaign, thousands of people, old and young, attended the mass meetings that were held in local black churches virtually every night for five weeks. We prayed, we collected money, we teased the white policemen who had been sent there to spy on us. As the preachers got warmed up, the spiritual energy got hotter and hotter. Both the source and the reflection of our soaring strength and unity was our music. The songs—"I'm on My Way to Freedom Land," "Oh, Freedom over Me," "Ain't Gonna Let Nobody Turn Me Around"—bound us into a whole that allowed us to accomplish feats we never would have been able to pull off as individuals and turned us into agents of what Dr. King liked to call "soul force." And so as you read the war stories ahead, try to keep the gospel tunes in your head. The civil rights revolution was a battle, yes, but it was also a profound spiritual transformation, not only of a people but of a nation.

Little Diane McWhorter was living in Birmingham only a few miles away from me but a world apart. In Sunday school, she sang "Jesus Loves the Little Children, All the Children of the World," yet as a white girl she was forbidden by the state, as well as by her society, to associate with children of what was sometimes called the "opposite race." It is a sign of the spiritual transformation I speak of that Diane and I ended up here on the same page: that she came to understand that my story is her story, too.

When "young folk" like Diane come around to interview me about the Movement days, they want to know how I could have been so "brave"—how I could have literally tried to get myself killed. (Of course there were some people who accused me of being just plain crazy.) I tell them, "I don't think of it as courage. I think of it as 'what one must do.'" There is a saying that the world will be changed by people whom the world itself cannot change. Those people are the "must-doers," and it was my honor and privilege to have been among them.

I discovered what I must do on Christmas of 1956. Right after the bombing, the baby of my four children, six-year-old Carolyn, came over to me and said, "They can't kill us, can they, Daddy?"

"No, darlin'," I said, "they can't kill hope."

[7]

THE MYSTERIOUS WAYS OF HISTORY

At the age that many of you are now, I found myself at the crossroads of history. The "crossroads of history" turns out to be one of those places that many visit but few recognize, except in hindsight. This was certainly true of me when my hometown of Birmingham, Alabama, became a landmark of the civil rights movement, the site of the turning-point battle in the long African-American struggle for freedom.

That was back in 1963. For the previous seven years, the Reverend Dr. Martin Luther King Jr., a black Baptist minister from Atlanta, Georgia, had been leading a movement to liberate his people from the nearly century-old after-

Author Diane McWhorter, sixth grade, 1963

math of slavery: segregation. This brutal system of laws and customs shut African Americans out of the social mainstream and denied them their full humanity.

Birmingham was considered the most segregated city in America—which explained why King brought the civil rights movement there at the urging of Fred Shuttlesworth in the spring of 1963. Black children my age marched in protest of segregation. City officials sicced police dogs and turned fire hoses on them. Photographs of that electrifying confrontation became famous worldwide. They shocked the conscience of the nation and helped push the government to abolish segregation.

I didn't see those pictures or grasp the significance of what they revealed. (My local newspaper refused to print them, but you can see them on pages 82 and 83.) From my point of view, as a white child of privilege, the civil rights movement was unfairly giving our self-anointed Magic City a bad name.

Here's how things looked from my side of the civil rights revolution:

1. I thought Martin Luther King was an "outside agitator" and that he had come to Birmingham to stir up our black people so that he could get rich. I saw no difference between the nonviolent demonstrations King was leading and riots.

2. According to the white adults around me, the fire hoses and police dogs that the city used against black demonstrators were "kinder than bullets." (But even I didn't believe the stories that the protesters had stuffed T-bone steaks under their clothes to make the dogs attack them.)

3. I couldn't tell you then what *civil rights* meant, but grown-ups sounded so disgusted when they mentioned them that I figured they had to be bad words. My father was slipping out at night to attend what he called "civil rights meetings." In my culture, it was understood that civil rights meetings were where people arranged to stop the civil rights movement. I hoped that my father wouldn't do something illegal that would make me the object of gossip at school.

4. One of the burning questions of my sixth-grade class that year was "Are you prejudiced?" (No one needed to ask whom the prejudice was against: "colored people,"or "Negroes," as African Americans were called back then.) A lot of my friends admitted that, yes, they were. But I had landed on what I considered a brilliant moral position. "I'm a white supremacist," I said, "but I'm not *prejudiced* against them." I thought that it was possible to be part of a totally anti-democratic, dehumanizing social order without being ugly about it. Indeed, southern whites took pride in how "good" we were to "our colored people."

I wish I could tell you that all this was shocking and exceptional. But my attitudes were wholly average for my time and place. I was a nice girl growing up in a polite setting, being groomed for a fine college and a future as a productive citizen. The oppression of African Americans around me did not strike me as having anything to do with my life.

The wonder of it all is that the child segregationist I was became an adult who devoted 19 years to writing about the end of segregation in

[9]

America. By the time my book *Carry Me Home* was published in 2001, the late Dr. King was a national hero, with his own federal holiday. My children had begun celebrating his memory at such a young age that my daughter Lucy, then a kindergartner, asked me why I insisted on referring to him as "King" when his last name was "Junior." Meanwhile, her younger sister, Isabel, came home from nursery school on the week of the King holiday singing an anthem whose words she thought were "We shall overclum."

In the course of my daughters' early education about the civil rights movement, I began to wonder whether they were much better informed about what had happened than I had been at their age. For one thing, they had the impression that the Movement was a one-man show, with King singlehandedly leading his people to the Promised Land (once Rosa Parks had refused to give up her seat on the bus, that is). They seemed to think that King had whipped segregation simply by being "nice."

As for their understanding of segregation itself, my girls knew about "colored" water fountains and "the back of the bus," but had no real concept of the mind-boggling, soul-piercing, spirit-numbing, body-bruising injustice that black Americans faced not so very long ago here in the land of the free. The message my daughters were getting was that the country had gone through some temporary insanity, but thanks to Martin Luther King, we had come to our senses.

I hope this book will leave you with an understanding that the dream of freedom— African Americans' hard passage from slavery to what the Movement song called Freedom Land— is the core struggle between power and justice in our nation. I hope you will gain a new appreciation of the famous footage of King's "I Have a Dream" speech. Many people—extraordinary and ordinary, courageous and scared, a lot of them children—made it possible for King to claim that immortal podium.

Just as important, I hope this history will make you feel outraged at those who stood in the way of their fellow human beings' liberty. While I want you to identify with the heroes of the civil rights era, I urge you also to imagine yourselves in the place of those villains. Perhaps the hardest thing to understand about the segregationists is that most of them were just average people caught up in behavior that mocked their own ideals.

What you are about to read goes against our national self-portrait of fairness. (Be warned, you will hear whites using the word *nigger* in these pages; to sanitize the language of segregation is to mute its destructive force.) As disturbing as some of the material in this book is, it will enable you to appreciate the hardships faced by those without power and to admire their strength to overcome so much.

Americans tend to cast the racism of the South as a separate world. But you will notice something as you read about the civil rights struggle after it moved from the South's blunt cruelty to the gentler malice of the North. The South was not a contradiction of America; it was a magnifying mirror. It made vivid the values that were elsewhere veiled or abstract. Segregation in the South was a literal, legalized version of the discrimination that hampered African Americans throughout the country.

Segregation's clear-cut injustices meant that the average Southerner—children included—constantly confronted moral dilemmas that had never even come up in most people's lives. As a

The author, second from right, with her Camp Fire Girl troop

child, I drank the cool water from the white folks' fountain (the "colored" water was usually lukewarm), even though I knew it was wrong.

But now I feel almost privileged to have grown up in the wrong place at the wrong time. The path my own life has taken since is an example of what the African-American writer James Baldwin meant when he said, "People are trapped in history, and history is trapped in them." I was a member of the last generation to grow up under segregation, and so my personal identity contained the history of my Magic City, the American capital of segregation.

It took me nearly two decades, longer than King's career lasted, to research and write the story of the civil rights movement, to piece together the historic upheaval I had misunderstood while I was living through it. But in the journey back to my segregated past, I got to cross "the color line" and honor the American heroes who had been on the right side of the revolution. Now I can introduce them to you.

[11]

THE WORLD UNMADE BY THE MOVEMENT

*"It is not well to forget the past. Memory was given to man for some wise purpose.
The past is . . . the mirror in which we may discern the dim outlines of the future. . . .
Well the nation may forget, it may shut its eyes to the past, and frown upon any who may do otherwise, but
the colored people of this country are bound to keep the past in lively memory till justice shall be done them."*

—Frederick Douglass, former slave, abolitionist (1817–1895)

In the pages that follow, you will read about the thrilling democratic uprising that redefined America in the mid-twentieth century: the civil rights movement. The Movement, as it was often called, pressed our country to make good on its founding claim that "all men are created equal." Finally the rights of citizenship would extend to the large minority of Americans whose ancestors arrived here some 300 years earlier on slave ships.

To appreciate the transforming achievement of the civil rights movement, you need to understand the vast social evil it overcame. Segregation was a surreal conspiracy of law, politics, economics, and tradition that trapped black Americans in a lowly corner of society. Segregation deprived African Americans of the freedom that, as Martin Luther King Jr. put it, should have been theirs at birth.

SEPARATE AND TOGETHER

Though black Americans were discriminated against throughout the country, their personhood was most systematically violated in the South. For a black or white child growing up there before 1964, the most tragic thing about this segregated world was that eventually it would start to feel normal. If you were white, you accepted that your black housekeeper—even though she took care of you like a second mother—had a separate, plastic drinking cup in the pantry. She cooked your meals but never sat down and ate them with you. You knew not to "yes, ma'am" her or refer to any black woman as a "lady."

On shopping trips to local department stores, you saw black families lined up to use the small bathroom behind the door marked "COLORED." Many stores didn't provide restrooms for their black customers, which explained why you some-times spotted a well-dressed black woman on the sidewalk clutching the hand of her child as he urinated in the gutter. Black people were also for-bidden to try on clothes before buying them.

You got a glimpse of a foreign, black-only uni-verse when you went with your mother to drive the maid home. (Occasionally the buses weren't running, and on the wages your parents paid her, the maid couldn't buy a car. She welcomed dis-carded furniture and appliances from your household, too.) Driving into her neighborhood on the other side of town, you instinctively rolled up the car window. Some streets were unpaved, and the yards were dirt. From the look of things, garbage pick-up was unreliable.

Although polite white children were forbid-den to use the word *nigger*, it was acceptable to refer to this bleak, crowded neighborhood (where your arrival was keenly noticed) as "nig-

gertown." Somehow you held the residents responsible for its sorry condition, as the white South in general blamed African Americans for the low status it had imposed upon them.

Robed Klansmen walk in downtown Montgomery, Alabama, prior to a cross-burning rally in 1956. Flyers advertising the Klan meeting read, "We believe in white supremacy. We need you—you need us."

THE "PLACE" OF BLACK FOLK

Black behavior under segregation was all about "knowing your place" and not acting "uppity." Your place was the back of the bus, the balcony of the movie theater, and the colored waiting room. If you were trying to get service in a store, all white people would be helped before you, even if they had arrived after you. Your father tipped his hat to any passing white person. He "yes, sirred" or "yes, ma'amed" the whites who addressed him as "boy" or, if he had gray hair, "uncle." It was dangerous to ignore the rules. During World War II, two black soldiers were murdered in Mississippi by a group of white men to whom they had said "yes" instead of "yes, sir."

If you were black and male, you knew not to look white folks directly in the eye after you reached a certain age. You moved off the sidewalk when whites approached. You made no comment about the appearance of a white female. In small towns where it was not uncommon for young black and white children to play together, those relationships ended before puberty. You now had to address your former white friends as, say, "Mr. Sid" or "Miss Sally."

The white South was obsessed with the taboo against intimacy between black men and white women, which might lead to the mixing of the races, popularly known as "mongrelization." (There was no such rule barring white men from black women; many plantation owners had fathered children with their slaves.) If you wanted a visual aid to show how white Southerners liked "their" black men to be, the town of Natchitoches, Louisiana, had erected a bronze statue of the "good darkie," holding his hat in his hand and respectfully bowing his head.

THE SEGREGATED MIND

At some point, nearly all southern children witnessed firsthand the cruelty of segregation. For whites, it might have been seeing a beloved caretaker barred from accompanying the family into a restaurant because she was not wearing a servant's uniform, or watching a black mother scold her little girl for unknowingly taking a "white" seat on the bus. For black youngsters, the trigger was often the local amusement park, where only white families could enjoy the lit-up rides. From that moment of recognition, Southerners of both races had to live with a split, segregated consciousness. They began to accept a form of social insanity as reasonable.

White Southerners thought of themselves as

[15]

HARRIET TUBMAN: SLAVE EMANCIPATOR

Perhaps the earliest organized civil rights movement was the Underground Railroad, a network of hiding places, tunnels, and human helpers of both races (but no actual trains) through which slaves escaped from the South to freedom. Its most successful "conductor" was Harriet Tubman, an escaped slave born around 1820 in Maryland, who made a record 19 trips south, liberating more than 300 slaves.

[16]

THE BEGINNINGS OF SEGREGATION

How did a system so blatantly unjust come to thrive in a country created on the principle of equality? Segregation—racism made into law—spread throughout the South after the U.S. government abandoned its attempts to reform the Confederate states following the Civil War.

Racism operated on many levels—emotional, psychological, political, and social. But because segregation was in some way a replacement for slavery, and the purpose of slavery was to provide cheap labor for the South's cotton plantations, it stands to reason that one of the most powerful arguments for segregation was economic.

Segregation served the rich and powerful by driving a wedge between the poor blacks and poor whites, who together vastly outnumbered them. The elite actively fanned racial tension by appealing to the poor white man's shame—his fear that he might not be any better than a former slave. As long as rich and poor whites were united against poor blacks in a brotherhood of white supremacy, there was no danger that the

good people and faithful churchgoers. In their limited contact with black people, most whites believed that they were kind and decent. The highest praise a white southern male could receive was to be called "a fine Christian gentleman." Yet this term was invariably used to insist that being a segregationist did not make one immoral. For white people, trying to reconcile segregation with their Judeo-Christian heritage warped their conscience and blurred their moral vision. Just as white people came to claim a superiority to which they were not entitled, black people began to believe in the inferiority inflicted on them from the outside.

THE BROKEN PROMISE OF EMANCIPATION AND RECONSTRUCTION

The Civil War turned out to be only the beginning of African Americans' fight for freedom. Initially, the Union government gave hope to its black citizens. It abolished legal slavery in 1865 through the 13th Amendment to the Constitution. In 1868, it guaranteed African Americans equal rights and equal protection under the law with the 14th Amendment. The 15th Amendment (1870) gave black men the right to vote.

The federal government tried to remake the South into a real democracy during the Radical Reconstruction era (1867–1877). U.S. soldiers were posted throughout the former Confederacy to back up the rights of freedmen. Black men functioned as citizens and were elected to office, including 2 to the Senate and 14 to the House of Representatives. But blacks remained economically enslaved to the large landholders who had once owned them. Now "sharecroppers," the freedmen farmed the fields for a share of the cotton crop, which never produced enough income to pull them out of debt to their masters. Early on, it was clear that economic opportunity was an essential ingredient of freedom—the one that would prove hardest to get.

White southern Democrats fought to overthrow the Republican Reconstruction state governments. They called their return to racist normalcy "Redemption." The most aggressive Redeemers had been a secret organization of "true blue" Southerners called the Ku Klux Klan. Klan members hid their identities under hoods and sheets. They mutilated, killed, or otherwise bullied freedmen and their transplanted northern Republican allies, known as "carpetbaggers." Klan terrorism remained a key method of enforcing the racist order.

By 1877, the Democrats were back in charge of the southern states. The federal government deserted the slaves it had freed and left the South to its own devices. It would take nearly 75 years for the freedmen's descendants to woo the government back to their side.

have-nots would form a biracial alliance and do something radical, such as try to "redistribute the wealth." Historians are still debating about who and what were behind the legal separation of the races through segregation. But whether or not the economic powers created segregation (as they had slavery), it certainly would not have endured if it had not served their interests.

Around 1890, the southern states began passing the segregation laws that severely restricted where African Americans could put their bodies. They were banished behind the so-called "color line" to separate railroad cars, the backs of streetcars, the basements of hospitals, and inferior schools, hotels, restaurants, waiting rooms, swimming pools, ambulances, taxicabs, toilets, and drinking fountains, if any. Cities passed zoning laws limiting blacks to humble neighborhoods. Some southern towns banned them altogether.

Those were the "rational" restraints. In certain cities, black- and white-owned cars had to be parked in separate lots. Black witnesses in court were sworn in on bibles marked "COLORED." School textbooks reused from year to year were stored in different warehouses. White prisoners on death row were spared the company of similarly doomed blacks. A laundry service in Birmingham, Alabama, boasted on its delivery cars: "We Wash for

[18]

THE END OF THE BLACK VOTE

A top priority for white Southerners was to disfranchise African Americans—take away their right to vote, or their "franchise," and thus the political power they had acquired during Reconstruction. (Mississippi was the first state to disqualify black voters, in 1890.) The main way this was accomplished was through the poll tax. In Alabama, for example, a would-be voter had to pay $1.50 each year in order to vote. If he registered to vote for the first time when he was 40, he had to pay $28.50 to cover all the years back to 21, the age of eligibility. The poll tax knocked out 98 percent of Alabama's voting-age blacks. On top of paying the poll tax, a voter also had to own property, pass a literacy test, and have no arrest record. By 1948, 7.7 million potential southern voters, black and white, had been disqualified.

White People Only." That city had also passed a law specifically forbidding blacks and whites to play checkers together. The craziest law came out of South Carolina: Black cotton-mill workers could not look out the same windows as the white workers. The segregationists had gone so far as to claim ownership of the air.

There had to be strong emotion beyond the practical economic considerations that moved otherwise reasonable people to such incredible behavior. The cultural paranoia behind segregation was the fear that black men were bent on raping white women. Making sure that this ultimate "color line" was never crossed had both inspired and provided the justification for the South's harshest custom: lynching. This was the fool-proof method of keeping blacks "in their place."

SEPARATE BUT EQUAL

In 1892, a 30-year-old New Orleans shoemaker named Homer Plessy agreed to help a committee of minorities test the constitutionality of segregation. Seven out of his eight great-grandparents were white; but Plessy was officially a Negro in the South, where legislatures would soon pass laws defining blackness by "one drop of blood." On June 7, Plessy boarded a train, took a seat in

In this cartoon from 1874 a member of the "White League" shakes hands with a Ku Klux Klan member.

[19]

the white-only car, and (according to plan) was arrested for violating the local law that restricted his race to its own car. His subsequent conviction was appealed all the way to the Supreme Court. The landmark case was called *Plessy v. Ferguson*.

In 1896, the nation's highest court gave its blessing to the South's "Way of Life." The Supreme Court ruled, with only one justice dissenting, that segregation did not violate the 14th Amendment's guarantee of "equal protection of the laws"—as long as the separate facilities provided for African Americans were "equal" to the white-only ones from which they were excluded. "If

LYNCH LAW

How did the white people frighten the southern black population into submission, especially in areas of the South where the whites were outnumbered? They had an ultimate tool of control over African Americans: a form of punishment without trial known as lynching.

Lynching was the community-approved revenge murder of (usually) a black male, often by upstanding citizens so proud of their handiwork that they posed for pictures in front of the corpse. The preferred killing ritual was hanging, and victims were routinely burned and castrated. The classic target was a black man suspected of having raped, or made any sexual advances toward, a white woman. But many times the actual "crime" was owning property, accumulating wealth, or otherwise showing independence or "uppitiness." It was equally dangerous for blacks to make

A sign outside of the NAACP

Ida B. Wells

a grab at political power: Lynchings of blacks peaked at 161 deaths in 1892 when freedmen joined with poor whites across class lines and formed their own People's Party (better known as the Populists) to challenge the rich Democratic politicians.

That year, Ida B. Wells, a fiery teacher-turned-journalist who had been born to Mississippi slaves in 1862, launched an anti-lynching crusade that some historians consider the beginning of the civil rights movement. Wells was writing a column for a black Memphis, Tennessee, newspaper in 1892 when three local black men were lynched. In her editorial, she claimed that the crime of black men raping white women was usually unsubstantiated and often a myth. She even implied that white women might voluntarily seek the company of black men. Wells's column so outraged whites that a local newspaper called for *her*

Lynchings like this one of 32-year-old Rubin Stacy in Fort Lauderdale, Florida, in 1935 had the atmosphere of a community picnic, children welcome.

one race be socially inferior to another," the Court said in defense of segregation, "the Constitution of the United States cannot put them upon the same plane."

Thus was established perhaps the most damaging precedent in Supreme Court history: the doctrine of "separate but equal." *Plessy v. Ferguson* would provide not only the legal basis for segregation but also a moral hook on which white Southerners could hang their guilt for the next six decades. Segregationists could claim, correctly, that all they were doing was following the law of the land. Little more than 30 years after the federal government had dedicated so much of its citizens' blood to freeing the slaves, it had just handed its approval to a new form of enslavement.

[21]

to be lynched. Wells fled Memphis, to devote her staggering courage to ending lynching.

Wells published a broad study of lynchings in the South, concluding that only a third of the victims had been suspected of rape. Many of those men, she argued, were accused falsely. She wrote for a New York paper and went out on a speaking tour that took her to England. Wells's exposure of America's shame to the outside world forced her own country to begin taking the problem seriously. As the future civil rights movement would also find, publicizing the evil of the oppressors was an effective way of bringing about change.

THE GREAT ACCOMMODATOR
VERSUS THE TALENTED ONE

This national spirit of white supremacy was reflected in the country's most influential black leader, Booker T. Washington. The son of a slave and an unidentified white man, he preached a policy of "accommodationism" from his power base at Tuskegee Institute, an all-black vocational school in Alabama. Washington believed that African Americans should accommodate themselves to, or make the best of, their segregated status and strive for excellence among society's lowly orders. With financial backing from whites, Washington had built Tuskegee to "uplift" freed people out of the culture of slavery by teaching them trades and crafts. His goal of economic self-sufficiency for his race was honorable. The catch was that blacks were expected to stake no claim on the white man's higher education, political power, or economic privilege.

In Atlanta, Georgia, on September 18, 1895, Washington delivered a historic speech embracing the notion of "separate but equal"—eight months before the Supreme Court's *Plessy* decision. His vision of a biracial society was this: "In all things that are purely social we can be as separate as the fingers, yet one as the hand in all things essential to mutual progress." He advised his own people: "Cast down your bucket where you are . . . It is at the bottom of life we must begin, and not at the top."

The Great Accommodator's most withering critic was William Edward Burghardt (W.E.B.) Du Bois, who would come to be known as the intellectual father of the civil rights movement. The Massachusetts-born, Harvard-educated black scholar and writer called Washington "the father

of lies." Du Bois's position was this: "The American Negro demands equality—political equality, industrial equality, and social equality; and he is never going to rest satisfied with anything less."

Du Bois was a legendary snob. When he was once congratulated for being Harvard University's first black Ph.D., he said, "The honor, I assure you, was Harvard's." His idea of

Booker T. Washington, the "Wizard of Tuskegee," believed that instead of "rights," which had to be earned, blacks had "duties" to better themselves within the system.

how to liberate his race was to train a college-educated "Talented Tenth" to lead the way into the social mainstream and then pull up the less resourceful behind them. Du Bois's campaign against the accommodations of Booker T. Washington ultimately led to the creation, in 1909, of the National Association for the Advancement of Colored People, the NAACP.

Du Bois's Talented Tenth elitism shaped the civil rights program of the NAACP, whose founding leaders included a number of whites. The NAACP's sophisticated membership lobbied Congress (unsuccessfully) to pass anti-lynching legislation. In 1915, the NAACP organized a protest against D. W. Griffith's Hollywood movie *The Birth of a Nation*. Now considered a classic, at the time this offensive celebration of the Reconstruction Ku Klux Klan was a key factor in the national rebirth of that nearly dead terrorist organization.

The revived Klan gained a large following in the North, which faced its own "Negro problem" as a result of a phenomenon known as "The

W.E.B. Du Bois and approximately 20 freedom-minded black activists met at Niagara Falls in 1905 to mount a challenge to the leadership of Booker T. Washington. This "Niagara Movement" would join up with sympathetic white reformers four years later to form the NAACP.

Great Migration": Hundreds of thousands of blacks had left southern plantations and moved to northern cities in search of factory jobs during World War I (1914–1918). The country had so embraced the privilege of white skin that in 1919, President Woodrow Wilson, a native Southerner, imposed segregation on the entire bureaucracy of the federal government. His successor, President Warren Harding, was sworn in as a member of the hugely popular Ku Klux Klan at a ceremony in the White House.

The NAACP had little effect on the hearts and minds of the general white population. Various other black liberation movements made no significant progress either. But the NAACP doggedly continued its chief mission: a courtroom campaign challenging segregation laws by filing suit against the institutions or states enforcing them. Its two main targets were voting and education, the rights that Du Bois had singled out as "necessary to modern manhood."

Adopting a strategy of "legalism and gradual-

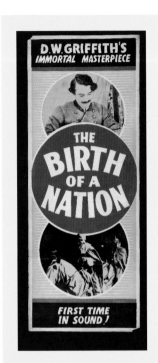

D.W. Griffith's movie glorified the Ku Klux Klan and prompted nationwide outbursts of white pride, including occasional gunfire at blacks on screen.

[24]

ism," the NAACP hoped to work within the court system to take apart segregation law by law and integrate blacks gradually into society. (Integration, or the attainment of full and equal participation for blacks in mainstream society, was the NAACP's goal.) NAACP lawyers scored important Supreme Court victories, overturning discriminatory laws in a number of states. But nearly 40 years after the organization's founding, segregation remained essentially unchanged. There simply wasn't enough manpower or money to take on every Jim Crow law. When the NAACP's lawyers succeeded in getting a law thrown out, the segregationists just wrote a new, improved one. It was like trying to empty the ocean with a teaspoon.

By the end of the 1940s, the NAACP realized that it needed a bold and different approach.

America, meanwhile, found itself at the center of a shift in world politics. Its once-ignored black minority moved into plain and urgent view.

By 1924, two years before this march in the nation's capital, the Klan had 4 million members nationwide. Klansmen totally controlled the governments of southern states such as Alabama.

THE COLD WAR

The end of World War II in 1945 brought America dramatic new global responsibilities. Suddenly the United States was a superpower, the leader of the free world of countries that practiced democracy. America entered a cold war with the Soviet Union, its former ally against Adolf Hitler and Nazi Germany. As the world's other superpower, the Soviets controlled the countries "behind the Iron Curtain" of Communism, with totalitarian dictatorships that did not answer to the will of the people. The United States saw its role as stopping the Soviet Union from gaining world domination. There was a threat of real, "hot" nuclear war between the superpowers, but the "cold war" referred not only to the arms race between the two countries but to their clash over values and economic systems.

In this battle of ideas, American racism was the best thing that had ever happened to the Soviet Union's anti–United States propaganda effort. America had set itself up as a moral example to other nations, but the undeniably anti-democratic treatment of its black citizens undermined its standing to condemn Communism. Ironically, the enemies of civil rights for blacks in this country, including important men in the

JIM CROW

"Weel about and turn about
And do just so.
Every time I weel about
I jump Jim Crow."

[25]

Though most Southerners referred to segregation as "Our Way of Life," the system also acquired the folksy name of Jim Crow. The original Jim Crow was a stage character created around 1828 by Thomas Dartmouth Rice. "Daddy" Rice was one of the "black face" performers who darkened their white faces with burnt cork and impersonated African Americans in minstrel shows popular at the time. The character Jim Crow was a lame and foolish old black slave who danced to the white man's tune. Rice's popular song-and-dance number was widely imitated in England as well as in America. It was said to be the first international minstrel hit, one of the more unusual examples of whites making money by humiliating blacks.

U.S. government, charged that the African-American struggle for freedom was a Communist plot. They accused those fighting to abolish America's most undemocratic feature of being un-American.

Added to the international drama of the cold war was a national development. World War II had brought on the emergence of a so-called New Negro. Historically, the aftermath of war had been a time of racial instability. In a six-month period after World War I ended in 1918, there were 26 race riots in American cities. Blacks were expressing their displeasure with second-class citizenship at home when their men had risked their lives on the battlefields overseas. White people put the blacks back "in their place" with 74 lynchings in 1919, the highest number in a decade. In the wake of World War II, after serving in a segregated military to stop the Nazis' slaughter of the Jews, African Americans were ready, as one black Alabamian put it, to take on "the Hitler nearer me"—the white supremacists on their own soil.

This was the context of the 1950s in which the civil rights movement bloomed in the dark heart of Dixie. Just as segregation had descended from slavery, this unexpected revolution was really the conclusion of the Civil War. Nearly a century had gone by since Frederick Douglass, the escaped slave-turned-abolitionist, persuaded President Abraham Lincoln to issue his 1863 Emancipation Proclamation freeing the

A segregated train station

SCOTTSBORO

The Communist Party promoted civil rights for blacks as early as the 1930s. The Party made an international cause of the "Scottsboro Boys," nine black youths falsely accused in March 1931 of raping two white women on a freight train. (Their historic nickname came from the Alabama town where the first of their 11 trials took place, resulting in death sentences.) After years of appeals, the "boys" were men by the time they were released from prison. Olen Montgomery (below, in overalls) and Eugene Williams (center) were freed in July 1937. By 1950, when the last Scottsboro Boy was released, the Communist civil rights pioneers were either in jail or in hiding because of cold war anti-Communism.

slaves in the Confederacy. A hundred years before Martin Luther King proclaimed his vision, Douglass, the first great civil rights leader, said, "I had a dream of freedom."

Here is the story of how the dream finally came true.

Frederick Douglass

[27]

BROWN V. THE BOARD OF EDUCATION

". . . I and my children are craving light—the entire colored race is craving light, and the only way to reach the light is to start our children together in their infancy and they come up together."

—Silas Hardrick Fleming, a parent suing the Topeka Board of Education, 1951

Kenneth Clark tests a boy's reaction to his dolls.

The four dolls were alike: baby dolls in diapers, bought for 50 cents apiece at a New York City five-and-dime store. The only difference among them was the color of their "skin." Two dolls were white; two were black. In the spring of 1951, the dolls and their owner, a 37-year-old African-American social psychologist named Kenneth B. Clark, boarded a train in New York, bound for destiny.

Clark and his wife, Mamie Clark, also a psychologist, had previously shown these white and black dolls to black children around the country as part of their research into the effects of racism on its youngest victims. When asked to pick "the doll you like to play with" and "the nice doll," a majority of the children chose a white doll. The next question was: "Give me the doll that looks bad." Most children handed the Clarks a black doll. The most chilling moment came when the psychologists asked the black children to identify which of the dolls was most like them. Forced to recognize that they were like the dolls they had rejected, some cried or ran from the room. But other children—all from the

[29]

THURGOOD MARSHALL: WARRIOR LAWYER

For a lawyer confronting the most serious problem in American democracy, Thurgood Marshall (pictured at center with two other NAACP attorneys in front of the Supreme Court) was funny, casual, and earthy. He was raised in a middle-class household in Baltimore, Maryland, the mischievous son of a schoolteacher and a blond-haired, blue-eyed African-American father.

Marshall attended law school at Howard University, the respected black school in Washington, D.C. His ambition was "to get even with Maryland for not letting me go to its law school"—on account of race. Winning admission for the first black student at the University of Maryland law school, in 1936, was his first school-desegregation victory.

[30]

headed by Thurgood Marshall, the country's best-known black lawyer—had sued a number of white state universities and won admission for black students. But even those successful cases had not challenged the legal basis for segregation: the *Plessy v. Ferguson* doctrine of "separate but equal." The NAACP had simply proven that the education offered to blacks by the schools being sued was either unequal or nonexistent.

South—had accepted their inferiority. One little boy pointed to a black doll and said, laughing, "That's a nigger. I'm a nigger."

When the National Association for the Advancement of Colored People (NAACP) discovered the Clarks' research, the country's leading civil rights organization thought it had found the magic bullet to slay segregation. For four long decades, the NAACP had pursued its strategy of "legalism and gradualism" to gain African Americans access to the polls and higher education. The NAACP Legal Defense Fund, Inc.—now

In 1950, Marshall made a major tactical shift: Why not argue that segregation itself was unconstitutional, that "separate" could never be "equal"? The NAACP was now going for all or nothing. It needed Kenneth Clark's dolls to win.

DOGHOUSE EDUCATION

In May 1951, Clark and his dolls took the train from his home in New York City to South

Carolina, where a group of black families from wretchedly poor Clarendon County was suing the state over schooling so awful that the NAACP called it "doghouse education." Previously, Marshall and his team would have simply pointed out the inequality of the black schools: that Clarendon County spent $179 per year on each white student and only $43 on each black student. Now the NAACP lawyers set out to prove that the very fact of separating the black children from whites because of their race caused such psychological harm that a "separate but equal" policy was impossible under any circumstances.

Clark gave his test to some of Clarendon County's black schoolchildren. Again, the white baby dolls were seen as "nice" and the black babies

A black school in rural Alabama. One of the parents in the South Carolina lawsuit said that she would never have wanted to desegregate the schools if her children's classrooms had only had desks.

as "bad." Up to the 1950s, most legal experts thought that bringing "feelings" and social science into the courtroom was off the wall. As one of the Supreme Court justices had written in the *Plessy* decision, if blacks took segregation as a "badge of inferiority," that was their problem.

Of the three federal judges in South Carolina who listened to Clark describe the black children's tragic self-doubt, only one judge concluded from the research that segregation was "an evil that must be eradicated," or wiped out. That brave rebel, named Waties Waring, was outvoted by the other two judges, who simply ordered Clarendon County to make its black schools equal to the white schools. Thurgood Marshall had been expecting their negative ruling. He and the NAACP promptly appealed to the Supreme Court for a final decision.

TAKING ON TOPEKA
Clarendon County, South Carolina, was only one of the nation's 11,173 segregated school districts.

Linda Brown, foreground, attended the all-black Monroe School.

Not surprisingly, the NAACP was pressing several other school cases around the country. The same day of the South Carolina ruling, NAACP lawyers were on a plane to argue their next lawsuit, in Topeka, the capital of Kansas. Topeka was not in the South; that was a good thing in the eyes of the NAACP. The city's segregated schools and limited opportunities for blacks showed that racial discrimination affected African Americans nationwide.

Twelve black families were suing the Topeka school district. The NAACP had been rather surprised that the father who volunteered to put his name on the case was Oliver Brown, a shy railroad worker and minister with no history of activism. Brown wanted his daughter to attend the cheery nearby white school, with wall art showing the sun shining down on happy youngsters, rather than walk across dangerous railroad tracks to catch a bus to an inferior "colored" school. Brown had not even told Linda, his seven-year-old daughter,

[32]

about his decision, which would make her the most influential young student in America.

At the end of the Topeka trial in the summer of 1951, the local federal court ruled against Brown and the other families. The judges basically said they had no choice: Since *Plessy* had been the Supreme Court's decision, it was up to the Supreme Court to overturn "separate but equal."

The high court was ready to hear the Topeka and Clarendon County cases in December 1952. By then, school-desegregation lawsuits from Virginia, Delaware, and the District of Columbia were also on appeal. The Court decided to lump all five together under *Brown v. The Board of Education of Topeka.* Even though the original lawsuit was out of South Carolina, the justices deliberately chose to title this landmark case *Topeka* in order not to appear to be picking on the South.

Signs condemning Chief Justice Warren were posted around the South. This one is displayed by Georgia's future governor, Lester Maddox.

make up its mind about whether to end "separate but equal," a legal precedent that was, after all, more than half a century old. On Monday, May 17, 1954, Chief Justice Earl Warren pronounced the Court's fateful verdict: "To separate [black children] from others of similar age and qualifications solely because of their race generates a feeling of inferiority as to their status in the community that may affect their hearts and minds in a way unlikely ever to be undone. . . . We conclude, unanimously, that in the field of public education the doctrine of 'separate but equal' has no place. Separate educational facilities are inherently unequal."

This was the NAACP's greatest moment of triumph. *Brown* was a glorious correction in the moral life of America—and one that had been clean, bloodless, and executed in a court of law. But the victory would prove to be an unsatisfying one.

A most unexpected reaction to *Brown* was its unpopularity among many African Americans. To

HEARTS AND MINDS

It took a year and a half for the Supreme Court to

[33]

THE WHITE SOUTH REVOLTS

May 17, 1954, the day the Supreme Court outlawed school segregation, was known throughout the white South as "Black Monday." What made *Brown* so much more upsetting to whites than the NAACP's previous school victories was that this one would finally affect young children rather than college students. That raised fears that black and white young people, comfortable with each other from an early age, would grow up to see each other as romantic partners. The imagined results would be that classic white Southern nightmare: mixed-race children, or "mongrelization."

The region's smartest white lawyers began rewriting state laws to rid them of illegal racial language while still having the effect of keeping the schools segregated. With only a couple of holdouts, Southerners in the U.S. Congress banded together and declared that their states didn't have to obey *Brown*.

Mississippi struck back most viciously with an organization called the White Citizens

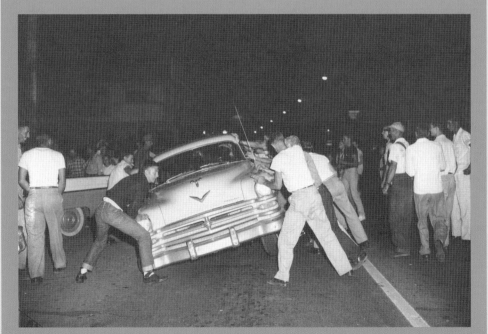

A mob in Clinton, Tennessee, whipped up by a White Citizens Council leader, attacks a car carrying African Americans in 1956, when the public high school there became the first in the South to be desegregated.

Councils. These councils tried to appeal to the South's "best citizens," prompting some people to call them the Ku Klux Klan dressed up in business suits, or "manicured Kluxism." Instead of physically roughing up those who wanted their freedom, the White Citizens Councils favored what one newspaper called "economic lynch law." They made it impossible for black people associated with the NAACP to find a job, rent a home, or receive a bank loan. As this white resistance spread through the South, critics compared the phenomenon to the rise of the Nazis in Germany 20 years earlier.

Despite the new economic face of lynching, there were still plenty of violent racists around committing old-fashioned murder. A year after the *Brown* decision, they would show the world that, for a black child in the American South, getting an education was sometimes less of a concern than staying alive.

Thurgood Marshall's dismay, southern black communities began planning "islands of jim crow schools" because the "privilege" of attending white schools seemed both an insult and a scary risk. As only a minority of black students would even want to attend white schools, one contemporary black journalist observed, "School desegregation does not involve the Negro masses." This statement spoke to the core criticism of the NAACP's Talented Tenth approach to liberation. *Brown* did nothing for African Americans beyond school age and, as the Supreme Court soon guaranteed, for very few attending school either.

A year after the landmark Supreme Court decision, not a single southern school had been desegregated. In 1955, the justices issued what became known as *Brown II,* their instructions for carrying out the original decision. The Court urged that the schools be integrated "with all deliberate speed." It was a phrase that would live on as *Brown*'s regrettable slogan. The South translated that time frame as "never." The Court had turned over the responsibility for school desegregation to the very states that, as Kenneth Clark's dolls had so heartbreakingly shown, caused millions of young black souls to dislike their own skin.

[35]

EMMETT TILL

"Let the people see what I've seen."

—Mamie Till Bradley, mother of Emmett Till, August 1955

Emmett Till with his mother, Mamie Till Bradley. Her family had been among the hundreds of thousands of blacks who left the South for northern cities in the Great Migration beginning during World War I. Chicago's black population grew from 44,000 in 1910 to 234,000 in 1930. Mamie Bradley's community outside Chicago was known as "Little Mississippi."

Emmett Louis "Bo" Till, a chubby 14-year-old mama's boy from Chicago, had been showing off his northern big-city ways to the cousins he was visiting way down in tiny Money, Mississippi. That hot Wednesday evening in August 1955, in front of a little country store, Bo flashed pictures of his schoolmates, among them a white girl he said was his girl-friend.

Egged on by his friends, Bo went inside the store and said "Bye, baby" to Carolyn Bryant, the 21-year-old white storekeep-er minding the cash register. Though the details of what happened next are a subject of debate, it is said that Bo followed his remark with a "wolf whistle." The black locals told Bo to clear out. Every black male in the South knew that to get "familiar" with a white woman was to invite the ultimate punishment: lynching.

Three days later, well after midnight on Saturday, Carolyn Bryant's husband, Roy, and his half-brother, J. W. Milam, pulled up in a truck to the unpainted three-room shack where Bo was staying with his 64-year-old great-uncle, Mose "Preacher" Wright. The men yanked Bo out of bed and put him in their truck. They drove him around for hours and beat him bloody. Finally, they took Till to the banks of the Tallahatchie River. There, on Sunday, August 28, 1955, Milam fired his Colt .45 pistol at Bo's head. Then the white men threw the boy's body into the river. A heavy machine part from a cotton gin was wired to Bo's neck so his body wouldn't float.

THE CORPSE

Most murders of African Americans went unpunished and virtually unnoticed in Mississippi, which had historically led the nation in lynchings. Between 1882 and 1962, out of 4,736 blacks and whites lynched in the entire United States, 538 of the African-American victims were from Mississippi. In the months before Emmett Till's visit, an NAACP worker in Mississippi and another black man were shot dead for trying to register blacks to vote. But the lynching of Emmett Till would not be ignored, thanks to the boldness of his mother.

Mamie Till Bradley was a 33-year-old government worker in Chicago with two hard-luck marriages behind her (Emmett's father was dead). She had warned her son about how to act around white people before he took the train south to the state of her birth: "If you have to

Mamie Bradley collapses as the body of her son, Emmett Till, arrives at the Chicago train station. "Oh, God. Oh, God. My only boy," she cried.

humble yourself, then just do it. Get on your knees, if you have to."

After the murder, the State of Mississippi had made the Chicago funeral director sign papers agreeing not to open Till's casket. But Mamie Bradley insisted on seeing her son's body. The sight of it hit her like "an electric shock": the monstrously swollen tongue, the right eyeball resting on his cheek, his nose chopped. Daylight shined through the bullet hole in his head.

Thousands of people lined up in tribute at the Chicago church where Mamie Till Bradley put her son's mangled body on view, dressed in his last Christmas suit. The horror of it made some faint and sent others into fits. *Jet,* a black newsweekly, published a picture of the corpse. It became an instant touchstone in African-American culture. The Emmett Till case unified black Americans far more than the year-old *Brown* decision had. Contributions poured into the NAACP.

"THAR HE"

Mamie Bradley had made "Emmett Till" a household name. The eyes of the country turned to Mississippi in September for the trial of Roy Bryant and J. W. Milam. There, the next shock of the case occurred. Mose Wright, from whose house Bo had been snatched, took the witness stand. Though the killers had threatened his life, Wright pointed his finger at Bryant, then at Milam, and named them as Bo's kidnappers: "Thar he," Wright said. They were perhaps the two bravest words ever spoken in Mississippi. For his own safety, Wright was whisked off to Chicago, never to live in his home state again.

Milam and Bryant were found not guilty. They later confessed to the crime in *Look* magazine, in exchange for a fee of $4,000. The killers became outcasts in the community. Southerners knew that murdering a young boy was wrong. They just didn't want outsiders to tell them what to do.

The Till case caused cracks in the southern landscape: lynchers were made to stand trial; a powerless black man stood to accuse them. But nothing predicted the earthquake of democracy that would hit the state next door only three months later.

Mose Wright identifies his great-nephew's killers.

[39]

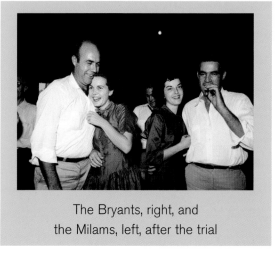

The Bryants, right, and
the Milams, left, after the trial

THE MONTGOMERY BUS BOYCOTT

"And you know, my friends, there comes a time when people get tired of being trampled over by the iron feet of oppression."

—Martin Luther King Jr., December 5, 1955

It was dark by 5:30 P.M. on December 1, 1955. The Christmas lights had been turned on in Montgomery, the capital of Alabama. A 42-year-old black seamstress left her $23-dollar-a-week tailoring job at a downtown department store. She boarded a bus for home. After a few stops, the bus was full. A white man was left standing.

Rosa Parks: "I wasn't frightened at all. . . . I don't know why I wasn't, but I didn't feel afraid. I decided that I would have to know once and for all what rights I had as a human being and a citizen, even in Montgomery, Alabama."

ordered blacks to give up their seats to any white person. So on this Thursday in December, the bus driver, J. Fred Blake, told the first row of African Americans to get up so that the white man could sit.

Three black passengers obeyed. The fourth sitting with them, the seamstress, defiantly slid over to the window and refused to go to the back of the bus. The black struggle for freedom had found the route into its future.

According to Montgomery's segregation laws, the very front of the bus was reserved for whites, and blacks went to the back. The middle seats were a no man's land filled on a first-come basis, used by blacks or whites as long as the "color line" was observed. But in practice, the drivers

That seamstress was Rosa Parks. In the legends that grew up around her, she came to be seen as a sweet, simple woman with tired feet who decided one day that she would not be moved. But Parks had been in training for this moment all her life. And the "tired" she felt was the kind of fatigue of the soul that has built for decades and finally sets off a revolution.

To understand how Rosa Parks's single act of bravery and rebellion became a turning point in history, it is necessary to appreciate the significance of buses in black life. In certain areas of their daily existence, black Southerners were able to avoid the rude reminders of their second-class citizenship. For example, no one was forced to go to a restaurant and eat behind a wall. But "the back of the bus" was a feature of segregation that most working black people, unable to afford cars, had to endure nearly every day. The white drivers cursed African Americans, slammed the door in their faces, drove past their stops, and even pulled guns on them. Parks's bus driver, who was from an Alabama town named, of all things, Equality, merely summoned the police to deal with his disobedient passenger.

"Why do you push us around?" Parks asked one of the police officers.

"I don't know," he replied, but took her to jail anyway.

THE TIME TO BE MENS

Rosa Parks was not the first person in Montgomery to be arrested for taking a stand against the bit-

ter insult of the buses. But she was the first one to have the maturity and experience to handle the challenge of being the symbol of a controversial cause. For years leading up to her arrest, Parks had been quietly fighting segregation by serving as the secretary of the NAACP's local branch. Her excellent reputation in the community served two important purposes: The segregationists would not be able to dig up any dirt on her, as they usually tried to do with other black activists; and her fellow African Americans were bound to rise up in outrage over her mistreatment.

Parks's boss at the NAACP had been Edgar Daniel (E. D.) Nixon, a gruff sleeping-car porter who was Montgomery's most outspoken civil rights leader. Nixon had grown impatient with the NAACP after receiving a reprimand from national headquarters for showing up with 23 black children at a white elementary school on the opening day of school after the 1954 *Brown* decision.

Nixon recognized that Rosa Parks's arrest was the perfect trigger for a new kind of protest. After bailing her out of jail, he summoned the city's black preachers to discuss taking action. When they appeared nervous about upsetting the white people, Nixon scolded them, "If we're gonna be mens, now's the time to be mens." He stated his bold plan: The entire black community of

[41]

WHY MARTIN LUTHER KING JR.?

Martin Luther King had many gifts that singled him out as the man of his moment, but two things immediately set him apart from civil rights leaders of the past: He was a preacher and a Southerner.

Most civil rights organizations, including the NAACP, were based in the North and were not associated with a religion or church. As a result, southern segregationists charged that "outside agitators" or Communists were coming down to stir up "their" black people. When the leadership of the civil rights struggle shifted under King to the southern church, it was harder (though not impossible, it turned out) to accuse the Movement of being a Communist plot.

Black ministers had the advantages of excellent communication skills (rehearsed in the pulpit) and access to a ready-made community of church members. Because their congregations paid their salaries, black pastors had economic independence that allowed them to take stands unpopular with whites. More important, the religion they preached gave African Americans the

[46]

strength to endure segregation as well as the courage to overthrow it.

In the past, black ministers had not been out front pushing for freedom. It was even more unusual for a man from King's privileged background to stick out his neck. Born in 1929,

Dexter Avenue Baptist Church

Martin Luther King Jr., right, is booked with his closest friend, Reverend Ralph Abernathy, for boycotting the buses in Montgomery.

Mike, as young King was called, grew up in a big house in Atlanta, Georgia. His father ("Daddy King"), the son of a poor farmer, had risen to become a big-time preacher, with a giant ego to match.

King graduated from one of the country's best black colleges, Morehouse, and went on to earn a Ph.D. from Boston University's School of Theology. This degree is what entitled him to be called "Dr."

Coretta Scott King, a northern-educated, classically trained singer from Alabama, who married Martin Luther King Jr. in 1953, greets her husband as he leaves court on March 22, 1956.

[47]

The most influential of the religious thinkers he studied, Reinhold Niebuhr, taught him that although an individual might be capable of good and moral action, groups of people behave selfishly in order to preserve their own power. That is what the slave-turned-abolitionist Frederick Douglass meant when he said, "Power concedes nothing without a demand. It never did, and it never will."

Throughout his coming trials, King for the most part kept his faith in the best democratic instincts of a country that had so abused his people. King matched Douglass as the rare prophet who held on to his revolutionary spirit, even as he became an honored citizen of the world. As one adviser said to him, quoting a Negro spiritual, "I have the feeling the Lord has laid his hands on you, and that is a dangerous, dangerous thing."

1957

Vote against
Integration!

HIGH SCHOOL STUDENTS
AGAINST INTEGRATION

LITTLE ROCK

"Smile, no matter what. Remember, not everyone approved of what Jesus did, but that didn't stop him."

—Lois Pattillo to her 15-year-old daughter, Melba, September 8, 1957

With her mother's help, Elizabeth Eckford made a beautiful dress for her first day at a new high school in Little Rock, Arkansas. She could not have known when she put it on the morning of September 4, 1957, that she would wear it throughout history in one of the most famous pictures of the civil rights era. The photograph shows the black teenager, whose fear and determination can be read behind her dark glasses, being hounded by a mob of equally well-dressed

Elizabeth Eckford, one of the Little Rock Nine

white girls and white mothers, their faces twisted with hatred.

Elizabeth had gotten separated that morning from the rest of the Little Rock Nine, six teenage girls and three boys who were the first black students to attend the Arkansas capital's Central High School. She had not been alerted to the students' group plan because her family did not have a telephone.

The night before, Elizabeth had read her bible, taking comfort from the 27th Psalm: "The

Lord is my light and my salvation; whom shall I fear?" Still, her knees shook as she made her lonely way past the jeering crowd down "the longest block I ever walked in my whole life." A kind-looking old woman spat in her face.

Elizabeth made it to the school entrance. There, she was blocked by uniformed National Guardsmen with bayonets. (The National Guard is an army under the control of the state that is called up in emergencies.) White spectators screamed, "Lynch her, lynch her!" One white woman, Grace Lorch, the wife of a teacher at a local black college, came to Elizabeth's rescue, accompanying her home on a city bus.

AUTHERINE LUCY'S REVENGE

This was a remarkable scene from many angles. Little Rock, proud of its reputation for racial harmony, had been the first southern city to announce its willingness to obey the *Brown* decision. Arkansas's governor, Orval Faubus, had been considered a political friend of blacks. Yet it was he who called out the National Guard against the Little Rock Nine. What may have prompted Faubus's rash racist stand was his concern

that he would not be reelected because of his previous racially progressive positions.

This was said to be the first time since the Civil War that a state had militarily blocked the will of the federal government. Thurgood Marshall and the NAACP lawyers involved in the case made the connection between this crisis and the Autherine Lucy case the previous year. They believed Faubus's defiance had been invited by President Dwight D. Eisenhower's failure to pro-

In support of Arkansas governor Orval Faubus's stand against integration, approximately 150 white Central High students parade through the business district of Little Rock.

tect Lucy at the University of Alabama (as well as his failure to hide his general displeasure with the *Brown* decision).

Neither Elizabeth Eckford nor the eight other black students got past the National Guard and the rabid adults that day, or for the next two and a half weeks. Their second attempt to enter Central High, on September 23, set off a white riot. The next day, President Eisenhower did what he had failed to do for Autherine Lucy: He sent in the riot-equipped 101st Airborne division of the United States Army, soldiers wearing the uniforms of war to take nine kids to school in an American city. Daisy Bates, a local newspaper editor, the head of the state NAACP, and a mother hen to the Little Rock Nine, walked onto her lawn, looked up to the sky, and saw the troops being flown in. "I heard the deep drone of big planes," she said, "and it sounded like music to my ears."

TORTURE CHAMBER

On September 25, the Little Rock Nine were carried to school in Army jeeps equipped with machine guns; helicopters chopped the sky overhead. At first, having paratroopers as their personal guards made the teenagers feel that democ-racy was working. ("Oh, look at them, they're so—so soldierly!" said Minniejean Brown, one of the students.) But that feeling didn't last.

Central High soon became what another student, Melba Pattillo, called "a hellish torture chamber." For the rest of the school year, the Little Rock Nine were called "nigger," threatened with dynamite or acid (squirted from toy guns), bombarded with firecrackers, slammed into lockers, and pushed down stairs. They occasionally cried, considered quitting, or verged on nervous breakdowns. "I wish I were dead," Melba wrote in her diary. Minniejean Brown, a target of particular meanness because she wanted to sing in the school chorus, finally called a girl who cursed her "white trash." Minniejean was expelled and was welcomed by a high school in New York. Printed cards began to appear around Little Rock: ONE DOWN ... EIGHT TO GO.

All eight black teenagers made it to the end of the year. When Ernest Green, the only senior among them, rose to receive his diploma at a graduation ceremony attended by police officers, soldiers, Daisy Bates, and Martin Luther King Jr., he was greeted with dead silence. It was an improvement, at least, over the slurs Green had heard throughout the school year.

[51]

Melba Pattillo, to the right of the soldier, desegregated Central High not because she was a crusader but because the school had "five floors of opportunities." Later she would say of her ordeal: "The only way I could get up those stairs was to say the Lord's Prayer repeatedly."

AFTERMATH

Civil rights milestones, like the desegregation of Central High School, often have the immediate effect of worsening the conditions they were intended to remedy. The fall after the crisis, the public schools did not open in Little Rock. They remained closed for the entire 1958–1959 school year. Children who could not afford private school or arrange to attend schools outside the city, including the seven remaining teens of the Little Rock Nine, lost a year of education. In the mean-

time, Governor Faubus was reelected by a landslide. A national poll selected him one of the ten most admired men in America.

For the remainder of the 1950s, the civil rights movement born with the Montgomery bus boycott searched in vain for a follow-up to that marvelous beginning. Black advances had only made the segregationists meaner. In Montgomery, the city government closed down all the public parks in defiance of a court order to desegregate them. Over in Mississippi, the White Citizens Councils practically ran the state government.

But even experiences that seem thankless at the time end up as landmarks of human progress. The Little Rock Nine are remembered as trailblazing heroes. For all their suffering, before and during the crisis at Central High, they went on to lead remarkably productive and successful lives. Melba Pattillo became a reporter for NBC News.

Ernest Green was an assistant secretary of labor under President Jimmy Carter. Another of the young men, Terrence Roberts, received his Ph.D. and taught at the University of California at Los Angeles. All are celebrated in Little Rock, though Elizabeth Eckford, a social worker, is the only one who made that city her home.

RUBY BRIDGES: LITTLEST SOLDIER

On November 14, 1960, in New Orleans, Louisiana, Ruby Bridges became one of the first black children to desegregate a white elementary school in the Deep South. Holding her mother's hand, six-year-old Ruby walked past a screaming mob of white people displaying a coffin that held a black doll. One of the four federal marshals escorting her was impressed: "She just marched along like a little soldier." The whites boycotted the school all year, with only a couple of white boys eventually coming back. Ruby did not realize that she was the cause of the commotion until one of the white boys told her, "My mom said not to play with you because you're a nigger."

Ruby Bridges

For months, Ruby walked past angry white crowds on her way to school, praying, "Please God, try to forgive these people." One woman addressed her in a high-pitched voice every day, "We're going to poison you until you choke to death." Ruby stopped eating everything but individually wrapped food items.

Ruby's teacher (a white Bostonian) welcomed her every morning with a hug. The following year, the white kids came back. Bridges's nieces attended the school more than 30 years later: Like many of America's urban schools, the one she had so painfully integrated had been resegregated. The whole student body was now black.

[53]

THE SIT-INS

"If it's possible to know what it means to have your soul cleansed—I felt pretty clean at that time . . . I felt as though I had gained my manhood, so to speak, and not only gained it, but had developed quite a lot of respect for it."

—Franklin McCain, one of the Greensboro Four

On the last day of January 1960, a North Carolina teenager named Ezell Blair Jr. announced to his mother, "Mom, we are going to do something tomorrow that may change history, that might change the world." Blair attended a black college in Greensboro called North Carolina Agricultural and Technical. On Monday afternoon, February 1, he and three A&T classmates, Franklin McCain, David Richmond, and Joseph McNeil, went downtown to Woolworth's department store, took a seat at

Protesters picket Woolworth's during a sit-in.

the lunch counter, and ordered a doughnut and coffee.

"I'm sorry," said the waitress, "we don't serve you here."

Though white-only lunch counters were a fact of southern life, one of the students replied, "We just beg to disagree with you." Before sitting down, they had deliberately bought some school supplies. Holding up a receipt, they pointed out that they had just been served at a nearby cash register. One of the most insulting hypocrisies of segregation

[55]

From left, Joseph McNeil and Franklin McCain, two of the Greensboro Four, stage a sit-in at Woolworth's. The store desegregated its lunch counter on July 25, 1960.

[56]

five-thirty, half an hour before closing time. "By then," McCain recalled, "we had the confidence, my goodness, of a Mack truck." In a week, the Greensboro Four had grown to hundreds. Within two months, protests had taken place in 125 cities in nine states.

A NEW DIMENSION

The sit-ins, as the lunch counter campaign became known, sparked a freedom flame that had been barely flickering since the Montgomery bus boycott ended in 1956. Between 1957 and 1960, there had been scattered student sit-ins mostly outside the Old Confederacy, but black colleges had never been hotbeds of activism. Critics accused them of merely turning out James Crow, Ph.D.s, black people who wanted to do well as opposed to do good. Yet it made perfect sense for college kids to take the lead. As Movement soldiers, they had big advantages over the grown-ups:

was that stores in the South, as Franklin McCain put it, "don't separate your money in this cash register, but, no, please don't step down to the hot dog stand."

The youths sat at the counter for an hour. They were heckled by a black dishwasher, and stared at by a white policeman. An elderly white woman cheered in a loud whisper: "You should have done it ten years ago!"

The store manager turned off the lights at

no job to lose, no family to support, easy communication with one another at school, hormones that made them fearless, and fewer years of absorbing the damaging effects of segregation. Plus, twirling on a stool at a soda fountain—an activity only white kids got to do—still seemed like freedom itself.

At the time, Martin Luther King Jr. had just turned 31. The main thing he and the Movement's other veterans had accomplished since the bus boycott was to form a preacher-led group of southern activists called the Southern Christian Leadership Conference (SCLC). SCLC's do-nothingism thus far had come to frustrate one of its founders, Fred Shuttlesworth, a hotheaded Baptist minister from Birmingham, Alabama. When Shuttlesworth visited one of the North Carolina sit-ins that February, he called SCLC headquarters in Atlanta, Georgia, the hometown to which King had recently returned. "You must tell Martin that we must get with this," Shuttlesworth said to the staff director, Ella Baker, "and really, this can shake up the world."

The sit-ins were, as Shuttlesworth said, "a new dimension." In the previous mass movement, the bus boycott, the protesters had not disobeyed the law they considered unjust; they simply stayed off the buses. This form of protest is called "passive resistance" because it doesn't confront the system head-on. What was different about the sit-ins was that the kids were actively disobeying segregation laws that they felt were unfair and immoral. This direct action, or civil disobedience, had been one of Gandhi's favorite methods in India. With the exception of Shuttlesworth, the ministers of SCLC had shied away from direct action, partly because if you broke the law, you might have to suffer the consequences and go to jail.

PROUD PRISONERS

For a black college student hoping to move up in the world, going to jail was especially humiliating because whites tended to stereotype blacks as criminals. But as the sit-ins spread outside North Carolina, and the police started making arrests, going to jail for the Movement became a badge of pride. One of the goals of Gandhian nonviolence was to "fill the jails" with political prisoners so that the unjust laws being broken could no longer be enforced.

Students had already taken over lunch counters in Nashville, Tennessee, as well as in Virginia, South Carolina, Maryland, and

[57]

Martin Luther King Jr., holding his two-year-old son, Martin Luther King III, observes a cross that was burned in his yard in April 1960 after the sit-ins spread to Atlanta.

particularly his father, Daddy King, who were trying to put the brakes on the protests. After much soul-searching, on October 19, 1960, King went with some college students to the Magnolia Room restaurant at Atlanta's finest department store and got himself arrested.

The jailing of King set off a national uproar. Massachusetts senator John F. Kennedy took time out from running for president to telephone King's wife, Coretta Scott King. (That gesture was at least partly responsible for swinging the black vote that won the presidential election for Kennedy two weeks later.) The pattern of King's career—and the dynamics of the civil rights era—had been established: King was the man who could command the spotlight and get the results. But he often needed the young people, like those lunch counter pioneers, to push him to the next frontier.

Kentucky when sit-in fever reached King's Atlanta. He found himself torn between the feisty kids and the more cautious older black leaders,

THE BIRTH OF "SNICK"

Once they launched the sit-ins, the students decided to organize into a movement that would take the struggle beyond the lunch counters and go after "more than a hamburger."

But should the students become a youth arm of Martin Luther King's Southern Christian Leadership Conference (SCLC), or should they form their own independent group? On Easter weekend of 1960, college kids from around the South came to a meeting in Raleigh, North Carolina, to sort out the future of the young people within the civil rights movement.

Some of SCLC's members, particularly Ella Baker, were critical of how their organization revolved around King. They were impressed with the students' "group-centered" approach, with no single person in charge and decisions made democratically.

Ella Baker, one of the creators of SCLC, engineered the formation of SNCC as a separate student group and remained its favorite adult adviser.

Although SCLC put up $800 to make the Raleigh conference happen, the 300 students voted to remain separate from SCLC and make their own way to freedom.

The new group they formed was called the Student Nonviolent Coordinating Committee. It would be known as "Snick," after its initials. SNCC became the most important Movement organization next to King's own SCLC.

For some of those present at SNCC's creation in Raleigh, the most memorable thing about that meeting was an old gospel hymn they had learned. Back in the 1940s, striking black workers had sung it on the picket line. It was a "powerful, welling thing," said one reporter at the SNCC meeting. Soon that song, "We Shall Overcome," became the anthem of the civil rights movement.

[59]

1961

THE FREEDOM RIDES

"When you go somewhere looking for trouble, you usually find it."
—John Patterson, governor of Alabama, May 1961

A burning freedom bus in Alabama in May 1961

It was John Lewis's first visit to Washington, D.C. It was also his first visit to a Chinese restaurant. Lewis was a humble Alabama country boy who had grown up baptizing chickens on the family farm before they ended up on the supper table. Now a 21-year-old ministerial student, he was a member of the Student Nonviolent Coordinating Committee's most impressive chapter, in Nashville, Tennessee. In May 1960, Lewis and his SNCC comrades had succeeded in getting the local lunch counters desegregated after leading a huge march to city hall. There the mayor confessed to them that segregation was morally wrong.

On May 3, 1961, a year later, John Lewis was starting out on a new history-making protest—though at the moment its participants were so worried for their safety that they were half-jokingly calling this Chinese dinner "the Last Supper." The following day began the next major chapter in the civil rights movement: the Freedom Ride.

The Freedom Ride was the brainchild of a

nearly 20-year-old civil rights organization called CORE, the Congress of Racial Equality. A small interracial collection of Gandhi-inspired radicals ahead of their time, CORE had staged restaurant sit-ins in Chicago in the 1940s. When the student lunch counter movement broke out in 1960, CORE stepped in to offer the kids some mature guidance. Stirred to mount a protest of its own, CORE decided to reenact the "Journey of Reconciliation" it had sponsored in 1947, in which its highly trained biracial team rode buses through the South to test a Supreme Court decision outlawing segregated seating on interstate buses and trains. In December 1960, the Court had expanded that ruling to desegregate interstate bus and train stations as well. CORE's new expedition—the Freedom Ride—would send 13 volunteers, black and white, around the South on regular buses to integrate the white waiting rooms.

The Freedom Ride was a departure from the direct action of the sit-ins. Whereas those lunch counter protesters were deliberately breaking segregation laws, the Freedom Riders were doing something that was perfectly legal. Yet they were also doing exactly what white Southerners liked to accuse civil rights activists of: "looking for trouble." As CORE's head, James Farmer, freely admitted, the Freedom Ride's aim was to get "the racists of the South to create a crisis." Only then would the federal government enforce the Supreme Court decision. In other words, CORE was hoping to get the white Southerners to attack.

"LUCKY" IN ALABAMA

Martin Luther King Jr. welcomed the Freedom Riders to Atlanta, Georgia, on May 13. Their first nine days on the road through the upper South had been uneventful. ("They heard we were coming and baked us a cake," a Freedom Rider said.) One of King's assistants told them that their luck would change once they crossed the state line into Alabama. Indeed, the next day, the first bus of Freedom Riders was chased out of Anniston, Alabama, by some 50 carloads of angry locals. A tire slashed back at the station went flat a few miles out of town, and a mob of white Alabamians rushed the Greyhound bus, waving chains and clubs. Someone heaved a fire bomb through the window. "Roast 'em," a man shouted. Bus passengers, not all of them Freedom Riders, threw themselves out the windows. Finally, an undercover state policeman on board pushed open the door, fired his pistol into the air, and ordered the crowd to stand back.

That set of Freedom Riders was taken to the hospital in Anniston. There was worse in store for the second freedom bus that afternoon when it pulled into the Trailways station in Birmingham.

Birmingham's Ku Klux Klan was the most violent in America, and it had friends in high places. One friend of the Klan was the city's most powerful elected official, Commissioner Eugene "Bull" Connor. Connor had assured local Klansmen that his police department would give them 15 minutes to assault the Freedom Riders before any city officers arrived on the scene. "I don't give a damn if you beat them, bomb them, murder, or kill them," a police detective told his Klan contact. ". . . We don't ever want to see another nigger ride on the bus into Birmingham again."

When their bus arrived at a little past four, the Trailways passengers—regular ones as well as Freedom Riders—stepped into an ambush of Klansmen armed with bats, soft drink bot-

tles, and lead pipes. James Peck, a white rider who had been on CORE's original Journey of Reconciliation, was jumped by five men. Peck was as "bloody as a slaughtered hog" by the time Fred Shuttlesworth took him in at his Birmingham church. Peck required 50 stitches in his head.

Commissioner Connor made a joke of the disaster. The reason there were no police on hand,

This picture is the only surviving shot of the attacks in the Birmingham Trailways bus station. Klansmen seized the film of the other journalists on the scene.

[63]

Freedom Riders John Lewis, left, and Jim Zwerg, a dentist's son from Wisconsin, took the first licks from the mob in Montgomery.

he explained, was that it was Mother's Day, and his officers were with their mamas.

KENNEDY'S INITIATION

The Freedom Ride was newly inaugurated President John F. Kennedy's introduction to the arena of civil rights. Front pages around the globe carried pictures of the charred bus outside Anniston and of the brutal thugs inside the Birmingham bus station, embarrassing the United States before the world community. Kennedy personally called Alabama's governor, John Patterson, demanding protection for the Freedom Riders. Patterson's position was, "We can't be nursemaids to agitators." The battered CORE riders gave up and hopped a plane to their final destination of New Orleans, Louisiana.

All except for John Lewis. Lewis and his SNCC friends back in Nashville decided that all would be lost if the Movement caved in to the segregationists' violence. Eight black and two white students wrote their wills and called Fred Shuttlesworth. Despite his warning that "you could get killed in Birmingham," they said they were continuing the Freedom Rides.

On Saturday morning, May 20, a bus carrying the new Freedom Riders left Birmingham for Montgomery. Another mob, this one including women, greeted them with shouts of: "Filthy Communists, nigger lovers, you're not going to integrate Montgomery." While coming to the aid of a white female rider, John Seigenthaler, a U.S. Justice Department representative sent down from Washington, D.C., was knocked out cold with a pipe. John Lewis was smashed over the head with a wooden Coca-Cola crate. He was lying bleeding on the street when the attorney general of Alabama, the state's chief law-enforcement officer, bent over him and handed him papers ordering an end to the Freedom Rides.

HELP

Martin Luther King arrived in Montgomery the next day. That Sunday night, an out-of-control white mob trapped King and hundreds of Movement supporters inside the church of his SCLC colleague Ralph Abernathy. The rioters threw stink bombs through the church windows. After a desperate phone conversation between King and Robert Kennedy, who was the U.S. attorney general, the Kennedys told Alabama governor John Patterson that if he didn't do his duty, they would send in the Army. Finally, Patterson ordered the National Guard over to the church to carry King and the black folks of Montgomery home in military jeeps.

The SNCC kids thought that King would, as they said, "put his body" in the struggle and join them on the freedom bus. His refusal dumbfounded them. He wanted to "choose the time and place of my Golgotha," the name of the site

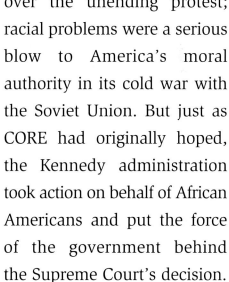

President John F. Kennedy, left, and his brother Attorney General Robert Kennedy, right, flank FBI director J. Edgar Hoover.

where Jesus was crucified. The students who had looked to King as their savior now referred to him mockingly as "De Lawd."

The Freedom Rides continued for months, though they never again caught the fury of their reception in Alabama. The Kennedys were irritated over the unending protest; racial problems were a serious blow to America's moral authority in its cold war with the Soviet Union. But just as CORE had originally hoped, the Kennedy administration took action on behalf of African Americans and put the force of the government behind the Supreme Court's decision. Attorney General Robert Kennedy ordered the federal agency in charge of interstate travel to issue a ruling that all bus and train terminals had to be desegregated by November 1, 1961. Direct action had gotten fast results, and the Kennedy brothers had just reluctantly entered the struggle that would define their careers.

[65]

THE FBI AND THE KU KLUX KLAN

The Federal Bureau of Investigation's job is to ensure the safety of the American public. But the FBI failed to fulfill its duty to protect the Freedom Riders in Birmingham, even though it was well aware that the Klan intended to bloody them up.

The FBI was paying an informant named Gary Thomas Rowe to spy on the Klan and gather information on potential racial violence. Rowe was an undercover member of Birmingham's most vicious Klan chapter, known as "Eastview 13." This "klavern" was in charge of the plot to beat the Freedom Riders. Thanks to Rowe, the FBI knew in advance about the planned attack as well as the Birmingham police department's role in it. But the FBI did nothing. Why?

The FBI's own informant Rowe—a burly, heavy-drinking bully known in the Klan as "Baby Brother"—had taken an active part in the beatings

Gary Thomas Rowe

at Birmingham's Trailways station. (He is in the right foreground of the photograph on page 63, with his back to the camera.) The local FBI agents covered up Rowe's crime so that they wouldn't get in trouble with their bosses in Washington. The FBI also let the other Klansmen get away with the mayhem, for fear that going after them (or stopping them beforehand) might blow Rowe's cover as an informant. That would have cost the FBI a valuable source of information.

This was the beginning of a long, complicated, and ugly relationship between the government and the Klan. Rowe would go on to escape punishment for other crimes. Meanwhile, the FBI's head—the powerful and spiteful J. Edgar Hoover—decided that the real danger to America was Martin Luther King. Hoover began a campaign of harassment against King that would last until the civil rights leader's death.

THE ALBANY MOVEMENT

"All. Here. And now . . . We want freedom now!"

—Martin Luther King Jr. speaking to the Albany Movement, 1962

At only 22, Charles Sherrod had been a sit-in veteran, Freedom Rider, and Baptist preacher, and was now one of the scrappiest, most talented members of the Student Nonviolent Coordinating Committee. In the fall of 1961, while SNCC concentrated on registering voters in rural Mississippi, Sherrod decided to expand its operations into Albany, Georgia, a pecan and cotton center that called itself "the tenth fastest booming city in the USA."

Whether out of fear or old-fashioned jealousy, representatives from the conservative NAACP warned Albany's townspeople that the SNCC newcomers were "Communists." But people

SNCC's Charles Sherrod, right, recruits local people into the Albany Movement.

showed up for SNCC's nonviolent workshops in church basements, and after about a month, nine students had volunteered for Albany's first sit-in. It took place on November 1, 1961, the day that the Kennedy administration's ruling in response to the Freedom Rides was to go into effect desegregating the bus and train stations.

Though the nine left before anyone was arrested, the sit-in set off a mass freedom uprising the likes of which hadn't been seen since the Montgomery bus boycott. Banding together under the Albany Movement, the town's African Americans decided they were going to stamp out Jim Crow: Their target was not just buses or

A DREAM OF FREEDOM

Albany's police chief, Laurie Pritchett (arresting Martin Luther King Jr.), was publicly the Movement's kindest opponent. In private he told Charles Sherrod that their conflict was "a matter of mind over matter: I don't mind and you don't matter."

lunch counters but, for the first time, the entire system of segregation.

THE EDGE OF SUCCESS

The new dimension the Albany Movement brought to the civil rights struggle was mass demonstrations, marches to the train station, to city hall, to the courthouse. Such protests are one of the freedoms protected by the Bill of Rights,

the ten amendments that were added to the Constitution in 1791 to make sure the government did not have too much power over individual citizens. In addition to the freedoms of religion, speech, and the press, the magnificent First Amendment guarantees "the right of the people peaceably to assemble" and ask the government to right wrongs (as the Kennedy administration did after the Freedom Rides).

Albany made national news on December 16, 1961, when Martin Luther King led a prayer march of 265 to city hall and was taken to jail. The Albany Movement had everything going for it—except success. The city officials stubbornly refused to consider any demands for desegregation. And Albany's police chief, Laurie Pritchett, was proving to be an unexpected kind of foe. He had read up on Gandhi's methods and knew that meeting the nonviolent demonstrators with violence would only turn them into heroes—as had happened with the Freedom Rides. So in the course of arresting the civil rights ministers, Chief Pritchett would politely bow his head and say a prayer.

Instead of coming to the aid of the civil rights protesters, the Kennedy administration congratulated Albany's segregationists for their gentleness.

The saying would go that Laurie Pritchett had "killed the Movement with kindness."

FAILURE

The campaign sputtered along for months, and infighting among the various organizations—SNCC, King's Southern Christian Leadership Conference, the NAACP—divided the once united Albany Movement. The media began to report the story not as one of black against white but of black against black. The city's refusal to make any concessions prompted one New York newspaper to call Albany "one of the most stunning defeats" of Martin Luther King's career. "We're tired, very tired. I'm tired. We're sick of it," King told Attorney General Robert Kennedy.

The Movement needed a testing ground where the segregationists would show the country their ugliest side. For King, that destination would be Birmingham, Alabama. But first, the Kennedy administration would finally confront the true face of southern racism, in the state of Mississippi.

[69]

Coretta Scott King gets assistance from Martin Luther King III, Yolanda Denise King, and Dexter Scott King packing a picnic basket for a visit to their father in the Albany jail. He had had himself arrested in July 1962 in an effort to boost the dying campaign. Chief Pritchett simply released him, pretending that his fine had been paid by "an unidentified, well-dressed Negro male."

1962

OLE MISS

"It was like watching the last battle of the Civil War."

—Dick Wilson, student body president, University of Mississippi

James Meredith, center, is escorted to the University of Mississippi campus on October 2, 1962.

James Meredith was not a typical civil rights figure, even though he became, in the fall of 1962, the first black student admitted to the University of Mississippi ("Ole Miss"). When Meredith had approached the NAACP about handling his case, the organization's top lawyer, Thurgood Marshall, said that any black man wanting to desegregate a school in Mississippi had to be crazy. Indeed, Meredith was his own audacious, unpredictable man.

Meredith was a 29-year-old husband and father who had tasted freedom in the 1950s while stationed with the Air Force in Japan. He applied to the University of Mississippi in 1961 after being inspired by the inauguration of President John F. Kennedy. When the Supreme Court ordered Ole Miss to admit a black student, Mississippi governor Ross Barnett responded, "Never!" Under the influence of the state's all-powerful White Citizens Councils, Barnett prepared for an uprising against the federal government—with bloodshed if necessary—that would force the country to wage war on itself.

Mississippians who were not in favor of such radical defiance were afraid to say so. The state had created an agency called the Sovereignty Commission that spied on and harassed citizens, black and white, who did not show enough enthusiasm for segregation.

President Kennedy and his brother, Attorney General Robert Kennedy, spent many hours on the phone with Governor Barnett trying to coax him into a gentlemanly solution. When James Meredith showed up for school on September 25, Barnett was on the Oxford campus to block him personally, "now and forevermore." After Meredith was turned away two more times, Robert Kennedy reminded Barnett, "Governor, you are part of the United States." Barnett replied, "I don't know whether we are or not."

WAR ZONE

Meredith was sneaked on to the campus on Sunday, September 30, 1962, and taken to his assigned dorm room. In an unreal display of calm, he read the newspaper. The Kennedys were hoping to protect Meredith with 400 non-military U.S. marshals. Wearing white helmets and yellow riot vests over regular clothes, the marshals stationed themselves on campus in front of the building known as the Lyceum (pictured on page 70, top left), where Meredith was to register the following morning.

Spotting the marshals, students began to chant, "Two-Four-One-Three, We Hate Kennedy!" By 7 P.M., marshals were being bombarded with lit cigarettes and gravel. Older, rougher men, who had come from as far away as California to defend Oxford, joined the mob of students. Their leader was an unstable former Army general, Edwin Walker, who had been commander of the troops sent in to protect the Little Rock Nine in 1957. Walker had later said that in Little Rock he was "on the wrong side."

Soon the marshals were facing Molotov cocktails (bottles filled with flaming gasoline), bricks, and iron pipes. Eventually there were shotguns, squirrel-hunting rifles, and a mob that numbered 2,500. At 8 P.M., the marshals returned fire with tear gas—the only defense they were permitted. A French reporter was shot dead at close range; a local jukebox repairman who had come to watch the action was fatally shot in the head. Their killers were never identified.

Just before 10 P.M., around the time James Meredith was turning in for the night, John F. Kennedy called out the Army. The president had

[72]

The crowd's emotional reception of Mississippi's Governor Ross Barnett at Ole Miss football games prompted comparisons to the Germans' hero-worship of Hitler.

bullets. It was a wonder the soldiers didn't fire on the mob. They marched across the burning ground without breaking step, thrusting their bayonets. Near dawn, the mob melted away into the mists of the tear gas that, along with the marshals' insectoid gas masks, had given Ole Miss the appearance of an alien planet.

BITTER VICTORY

On Monday morning James Meredith, dressed in a conservative suit and carrying a briefcase, rode in a bullet-marked government car across a campus littered with broken bottles and the corpses of birds that had suffocated in the tear gas. After Meredith registered, a student yelled, "Was it worth two lives, nigger?"

[73]

been forced to order what amounted to a military strike against his own country.

Governor Barnett directed the state police to block the highway into Oxford, Mississippi, forcing the Army vehicles to mow through the police lines. At 2:15 A.M., the first 117 U.S. soldiers finally arrived on the campus, their guns locked and loaded. The riot had grown so violent that 160 federal marshals had been injured, 28 of them by

In a stunning display of how far a state was willing to push the lost cause of segregation, a civil war had been waged in Oxford, Mississippi, 100 years after the first one. Against opposition it had underestimated, the federal government had readied 31,000 soldiers to defend a single black student.

But the war was not over. The battlefield now shifted to Alabama, for the coming "Year of Birmingham": 1963.

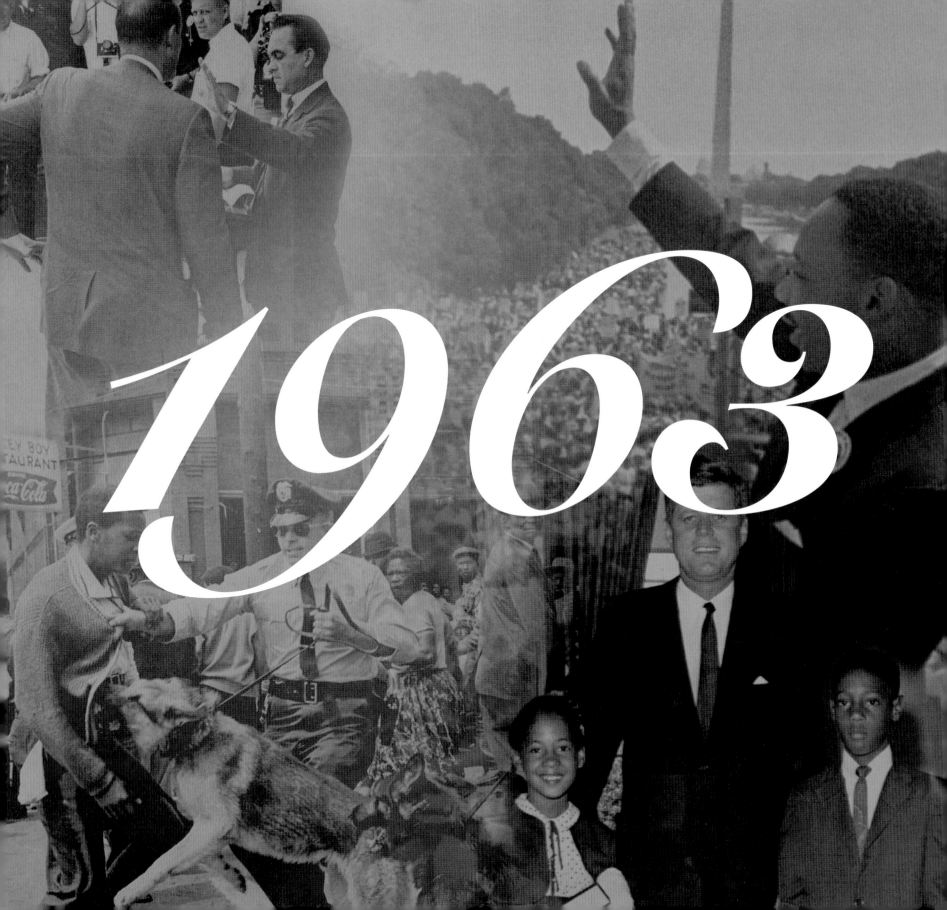

1963

BIRMINGHAM

"The whole world is watching Birmingham."

—Reverend Fred Shuttlesworth, SCLC leader, May 2, 1963

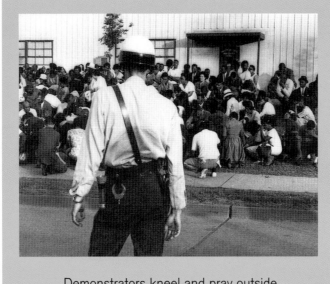

Demonstrators kneel and pray outside municipal buildings in Birmingham.

Though Martin Luther King Jr. considered Birmingham, Alabama, "probably the most segregated city in America," he had not wanted to take his Movement there: It was too dangerous. The man who had finally persuaded King to meet the challenge in the spring of 1963 was his most fearless colleague in the Southern Christian Leadership Conference (SCLC), Reverend Fred Shuttlesworth. For the past seven years, Shuttlesworth had been living up to his Movement nickname as "the Wild Man from Birmingham." Shuttlesworth had put his body on the line to fight segregation in a city he said had "a heart as hard as the steel it manufactures and as black as the coal it mines." His hometown seemed like the last place in the world whose soul could be saved by children.

Birmingham called itself the Magic City, but its black citizens had other names for it—the "Tragic City" and "Bombingham." Since 1947, there had been more than 30 bombings of African Americans' homes and churches in

FRED SHUTTLESWORTH: THE MOVEMENT'S BRAVEST

Fred Shuttlesworth grew up poor and ambitious just outside Birmingham. He decided that God had anointed him to free his people after Klansmen bombed his house on Christmas night of 1956. The next day, Shuttlesworth and his fellow activists went ahead with their planned protest, riding in the front of Birmingham's segregated buses.

The following year, at the time of the Little Rock crisis, he was attacked on a sidewalk by a white mob as he was trying to enroll his children in a local white high school. The legend would come down that Shuttlesworth, pictured with supporters after the assault, had announced to his attackers (who beat him with chains, the symbol of slavery), "I shall be dead before I will ever be a slave again."

Along with Martin Luther King Jr. and Ralph Abernathy, Shuttlesworth was one of the "Big Three" in the Southern Christian Leadership Conference. He was the Movement's pioneer of aggressive direct action, going to jail for freedom more often than any other minister. Shuttlesworth's confrontational spirit balanced King's gift for reconciliation. Both were essential for nonviolence to work.

Birmingham. Only one of these crimes was solved (and that happened because some black residents literally caught the bombers). Then there were the beatings and, most horribly, the Ku Klux Klan's castration of a black man in 1957, "to carry a message to Shuttlesworth." The conspiracy between the Klan and the Birmingham police to maim the Freedom Riders in 1961 had hardly been their only collaboration. The city commissioner in charge of the police, Eugene "Bull" Connor, had ordered or approved at least two assassination attempts against Shuttlesworth, including a bombing of his church.

THE PERFECT ENEMY

Bull Connor was just the loud-mouthed, nationally notorious white supremacist the Movement needed after being outfoxed by Albany's nonviolent police chief, Laurie Pritchett. SCLC would call its planned rendezvous with Birmingham Project C, for Confrontation. The aim of Project C was to provoke the segregationists into committing an act that would force the entire country to face the evil of segregation.

As it happened, the more thoughtful white citizens of Birmingham had begun to realize that Bull Connor was giving their city a bad name. In the spring of 1963, as SCLC was polishing its plans for Project C, these white people mounted a campaign to kick Connor out of city hall. On April 2, Connor was defeated at the polls. The following day, Project C began. In what would prove to be a lucky break for the civil rights movement, Bull Connor announced that he had no intention of leaving office.

Birmingham was SCLC's do-or-die campaign.

THE MAGIC CITY

Birmingham was the industrial capital of the Deep South. The steel mills, puffing like dragons on the western edge of town, were the key to why the city had become known as "Bombingham." The dynamite that went into the bombs was literally a tool of the steel industry: The iron and steel furnaces were fueled by local coal, which was blasted from the earth by dynamite. Many of the Klansmen involved in the bombings came from coal-mining backgrounds.

The miners' employers—industrialists known as "Big Mules"—had approved of Klan membership among their white workers: As long as the whites were fighting with their black co-workers in the mills, they wouldn't form strong labor unions and demand higher wages and more control over the workplace. The industrialists also published racist pamphlets that painted the labor movement as an international conspiracy of Communist Jews and their Negro dupes.

To do their political will, the Big Mules had gotten elected to city hall an uneducated baseball announcer named Bull Connor, who had gained regionwide popularity (and his nickname) by talking loud: "He's OOOOOUUUUTTTT!" Connor met his match in Birmingham's civil rights leader Fred Shuttlesworth. "He has to talk loud," Shuttlesworth said of Connor on national TV in 1961, "because when the sound and fury is all gone, there will be nothing. There will be emptiness."

[77]

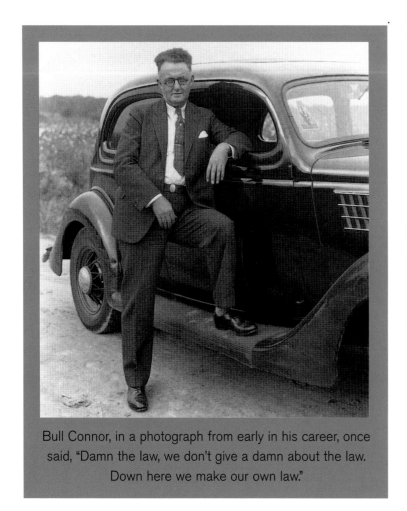

Bull Connor, in a photograph from early in his career, once said, "Damn the law, we don't give a damn about the law. Down here we make our own law."

So far, King's organization had piggybacked onto the efforts of others, mainly the Student Nonviolent Coordinating Committee (SNCC), for the sit-ins, the Freedom Rides, and Albany. The last was a failure from which King badly needed to redeem himself. The Albany Movement had made a mistake by taking on too large a task in its attacks on segregation in general. SCLC realized that it would be better to concentrate on limited, beatable targets. And those targets should not be politicians like Albany's city commissioners, who bowed to the will of the voters. They should be the businesspeople, who bowed to the almighty dollar.

Shuttlesworth and King decided to put pressure on the major department stores, where blacks were allowed to spend their money but were banned from the lunch counters and the restrooms (though some provided "COLORED" toilets). There would be sit-ins and picketing at the stores, but the centerpiece of Project C would be mass marches. These demonstrations would not only get the attention of the media, but would also strain the patience of Bull Connor's famously brutal police force.

STRUGGLE

For the first couple of weeks of Project C, however, the Birmingham police were as polite as they could be. Bull Connor, it turned out, had been taking lessons from Albany's Chief Pritchett, who had come up to Birmingham to coach Connor. Not only were the city's segregationists refusing to "cooperate" with Project C, the Kennedy administration had taken the position that King was being unfair by not giving

Birmingham's newly elected mayor a chance (assuming that Bull Connor would eventually agree to leave city hall). The Movement was also unpopular among many local African Americans, especially the prosperous middle class: They were afraid to risk what they had achieved within the segregated system—particularly on what was looking like a losing crusade. SCLC was having a hard time recruiting people to march because they were afraid of being fired by their white employers. The reporters on the scene were getting bored. Finally, in order to motivate the troops and jolt the news media, King decided he was going to have to go to jail.

The appointed day was April 12, 1963, Good Friday. SCLC had timed its campaign around Easter, partly because it was a season of intense shopping and thus an ideal time to boycott the department stores. For King to submit to jail on Good Friday would symbolically link his sacrifice to the crucifixion of Christ. Sure enough, as he led 50 double-file marchers out of church after noon that Friday, someone called out, "There he goes, just like Jesus." King, along with his closest colleague, Ralph Abernathy, Fred Shuttlesworth, and the other protesters, was arrested for violating a court order that forbade any further demonstrations. King's jailing finally got Project C on the coveted front page of the *New York Times*.

[79]

"You will never know the meaning of utter darkness until you have lain in such a dungeon, knowing

Martin Luther King Jr., right, was arrested on Good Friday with his favorite jailmate, SCLC's treasurer Ralph Abernathy, center. The Movement leaders had replaced their business suits with denim, not only to show that they weren't buying fancy clothes from the boycotted department stores but also to prove their identification with working poor people.

that sunlight is streaming overhead but still seeing only darkness below." King addressed these words to the eight local white clergymen who had published a statement in a Birmingham newspaper criticizing the demonstrations for being "unwise and untimely" and urging the black community to withdraw its support. King's lengthy reply, smuggled out of the jail by his lawyers, would live on as the Movement's most stirring statement of purpose and one of the sacred texts of democracy. But King's "Letter from Birmingham Jail" would not find fame until after Birmingham, and it did not rescue Project C from what appeared to be failure.

[80]

THE CHILDREN

During the week King spent in jail before bailing out, one of his youthful lieutenants, James Bevel, had a brainstorm about how to deal with the shortage of "jailbirds," as the protesters were called: Take the kids out of school and turn them loose on the streets. A former SNCC worker whom SCLC had hired away, Bevel was a civil rights figure such as Dr. Seuss might have created. He wore a Jewish yarmulke on his shaved head, even though he was a black Baptist preacher. He talked to the children as no minis-

ter had before him. "If God can feed the cockroach, he can feed the Negro," Bevel said. Or "The Negro has been sitting here dead for three hundred years. It is time he got up and walked."

EXCERPT

LETTER FROM BIRMINGHAM JAIL

You may well ask: "Why direct action? Why sit-ins, marches and so forth? Isn't negotiation a better path?" You are quite right in calling for negotiation. Indeed, this is the very purpose of direct action. Nonviolent direct action seeks to create such a crisis and foster such a tension that a community which has constantly refused to negotiate is forced to confront the issue. It seeks so to dramatize the issue that it can no longer be ignored. . . . [S]o must we see the need for nonviolent gadflies to create the kind of tension in society that will help men rise from the dark depths of prejudice and racism to the majestic heights of understanding and brotherhood. . . .

The kids went wild over Bevel's message. They were dying to march. But the black elders were scandalized. The Movement would be blamed if a child was hurt—or worse. Shuttlesworth sided with Bevel. King was still trying to make up his mind when Bevel summoned the kids to action on May 2. He was calling that Thursday "D-Day."

At least 800 kids skipped school and headed downtown to the Sixteenth Street Baptist Church, whose large sanctuary had been the staging ground for Project C. After freedom-singing and clapping and praying to "get their nonviolence," the kids filed out of the church in little groups. "Sing, children, sing," an adult spectator encouraged them. When the waiting police placed them under arrest, the children knelt like pros and prayed.

No movement in America had ever yet come close to achieving the Gandhian goal of "filling the jails" so that righteousness could no longer be punished. At the end of D-Day, more than 600 kids had been locked up. The children had scampered happily into the school buses pressed into service to handle the volume of jailbirds. Acknowledging that the system they were propping up was doomed, one policeman had turned

to another: "Ten or fifteen years from now, we will look back on this and we will say, 'How stupid can you be?'"

THE MIRACLE

The next day, Friday, May 3, 1963, was "Double D-Day." More than 1,500 kids were absent from school. Fire trucks had parked around Kelly Ingram Park, across from Sixteenth Street Baptist. The children poured out of the church into the park. A police captain ordered them, "Disperse, or you'll get wet." When some kids sat on the sidewalk, the firemen started blasting them with their hoses. Two hundred pounds of water pressure sent children skittering down the pavement or plastered them against storefronts. One girl was turned end over end.

The crowd of more than 1,000 spectators responded with horror—and a few rocks. Bull Connor turned to his police captain and said, "Bring the dogs." The police department's K-9 Corps made their grand entrance. One dog was named, ironically enough, King.

The German shepherds waded into the crowd, straining against their handlers' leashes. One of them bit a man on the leg, and two jumped on another man, ripping his pants leg

[81]

and breaking the skin. A seven-year-old girl was knocked over by a dog.

Compared with the cruelties that black people had long suffered in Birmingham, neither dog bites nor hose spray ranked very high on the scale of brutality. But they were enough to get the Movement's message out to the world. As one black businessman said to comfort a woman weeping at the outrage she had witnessed: "This may be the best thing that ever happened to the Movement."

That evening's TV footage of the watery "Battle of Ingram Park" was hailed by one Movement strategist as "television's greatest hour." But it was a still photograph of a police dog attacking 15-year-old Walter Gadsden—printed in newspapers across the globe—that would shame America into making good on its black citizens' democratic birthright. That's why Project C's biblical panorama of young people facing down the dogs came to be known as the "children's miracle."

[82]

ACCORD WITH CONSCIENCE
President Kennedy immediately sent down Burke Marshall, the head of the Justice Department's Civil Rights Division, to convince the white businessmen of Birmingham that they needed to reach a settlement with Martin Luther King. This

This photo, published in *Life* magazine, is a classic image of the civil rights era. It was taken by a white Alabama preacher's son named Charles Moore. Birmingham's fire chief, whose department was used to helping, not hurting, people, resisted this assignment from Bull Connor.

THE PHOTOGRAPH

As a catalyst for change, this photograph of Birmingham's police dog Leo attacking 15-year-old Walter Gadsden has been compared to Harriet Beecher Stowe's 1852 novel, *Uncle Tom's Cabin*, which turned public opinion against slavery. Taken by Associated Press photographer Bill Hudson on May 3, 1963, the picture electrified the country. President Kennedy said it made him sick. The snarling police dog reminded some of the Nazis' Gestapo. (Ironically, the K-9 Corps was "on duty" for less than 30 minutes during the five weeks of protests.)

Though one's impression is that Gadsden is meekly accepting Leo's assault, his knee is breaking the dog's lunge and he has grabbed the policeman's wrist. This amazing act of boldness inspired many local blacks. Though Hudson's photograph made white America feel the victimization of blacks, it helped African Americans overcome their fear of the police—an essential stage of liberation.

[83]

was no easy job: Most white Southerners regarded King as the devil, referring to him as Martin Lucifer King. But in their desperation, the white leaders agreed to negotiate. As one businessman put it, "I'm a segregationist, but I'm not a damn fool."

Tension had been building between King and Shuttlesworth during the long month of Project C, and it now erupted into a big fight. King, the conciliator, had had enough confrontation with the segregationists. He wanted to call off the demonstrations while the settlement talks were going on, before the Movement's demands had been met. SCLC was legitimately scared that its record of no serious injuries could not hold. Shuttlesworth, the warrior (and the only Movement leader to have been downed by fire hoses), fiercely refused. "Here in Birmingham, the people trust me," he said to King. "I've never

Jackie Robinson, right, the first African American to play major-league baseball, was one of the many famous activists drawn to Birmingham by Project C. Accompanied by former heavyweight boxing champion Floyd Patterson, left, he points to the damage done by the Klan's May 11 bombing of the Gaston Motel, SCLC's headquarters during the demonstrations. The bombing set off the first race riot of the civil rights era.

lied to them. And you and I promised that we would not stop demonstrating until we had a victory."

Before the split between Shuttlesworth and King became public, the store owners finally agreed to the Movement's deliberately modest demands: the desegregation of the lunch counters, bathrooms, and fitting rooms, and the promotion of a few blacks out of their cleaning jobs into formerly white clerical positions. At a press conference with King on May 10, Shuttlesworth announced, "Birmingham has reached an accord with its conscience."

Although the gains won in Birmingham may seem minor, Project C brought about one of the most dramatic shifts in the history of the country. The Movement—and, especially, those Double D-Day photographs—forced the country to admit that segregation was morally unacceptable. Martin Luther King, in turn, finally fulfilled the early promise of his leadership during the Montgomery bus boycott. As the Movement's victory inspired "mini-Birminghams" of protest around the South, President Kennedy mobilized the full might of his administration to bring about an end to segregation. "As Birmingham goes," King's aides had accurately predicted, "so goes the South."

STAND IN THE SCHOOLHOUSE DOOR

*"I . . . hereby denounce and forbid this illegal
and unwarranted action by the central government."*

—George Wallace, governor of Alabama, June 11, 1963

"**S**egregation now! Segregation tomorrow! Segregation forever!" Those were probably the most famous—or infamous—words ever spoken at the inauguration of an American governor. They were practically yelled by George Corley Wallace, a feisty former boxing champion, when he was sworn in as Alabama's top elected official in January 1963.

A crusader for the have-nots, Wallace had initially been "pro-Negro" for his time. But after los-

Deputy U.S. Attorney General Nicholas Katzenbach, left,
is halted by Governor George Wallace, right,
at the "Schoolhouse Door."

ing the 1958 governor's race to the Klan-backed John Patterson, Wallace had promised never to be "outniggered" again. The applause line of his successful 1962 campaign for governor was a pledge to "stand in the schoolhouse door" to prevent blacks from entering the University of Alabama, which had remained all-white since Autherine Lucy was driven out by a mob in 1956.

The time for Governor Wallace to make good on his campaign promise came in June 1963. On the heels of Martin Luther King Jr.'s international-news-making demonstrations in Birmingham that spring, a federal judge ordered the University of Alabama to admit two black students.

ANOTHER RECONSTRUCTION

President John F. Kennedy and Attorney General Robert Kennedy were determined not to repeat in Alabama the near civil war of the previous September at the University of Mississippi. The Kennedys found unexpected allies in Alabama's business community. Segregation, which had once been essential to the local economy, had become "bad for business." No companies, or their employees, wanted to relocate to a place where the schools might be closed. After receiving calls from Kennedy's cabinet, Alabama's major employers began putting pressure on Wallace to avoid "another Oxford" (Mississippi).

But Governor Wallace knew that the best thing for his career would be a grand showdown with the federal government. Southerners equated the U.S. government with the Union officials who had committed the "ancient crime" of post-Civil War Reconstruction against the defeated South. With that in mind, on Schoolhouse Door Day, June 11, 1963, Wallace planted himself in the doorway of the university's Foster Auditorium. This columned brick gymnasium was where the two black students, James Hood and Vivian Malone, were to register under the escort of Robert Kennedy's deputy attorney general, Nicholas Katzenbach.

Rumors have persisted over the years that the confrontation at the Schoolhouse Door was "staged" by Wallace and the Kennedys. And it's true that both parties understood beforehand what the outcome was going to be: Vivian Malone and James Hood were going to enroll at the university. But neither side knew how far the other was willing to go. Governor Wallace half-feared and half-hoped he would be arrested. The Kennedys knew Wallace wanted them to send in troops so he could say that Alabama had been invaded.

In light of the mob riot that had greeted James Meredith and Autherine Lucy, soft drink machines had been removed from campus so that there wouldn't be any handy bottles to throw. Shortly before 11 A.M., Katzenbach walked up to the schoolhouse door, flanked by 400 members of the news media. Sweat glistened on his bald head, and his leg shook from nerves. James Hood and Vivian Malone remained in the car.

Wallace halted Katzenbach with a traffic cop's palm in the face. The governor read his prepared statement, denouncing the "central government."

Katzenbach leaned forward. "The students," he told the governor, "will register today to go to school tomorrow." Act I came to an end.

DUTY

During the lunch break, the Kennedys decided to get it over with and federalize Alabama's National Guard, putting the state militia under the president's command. When Wallace reclaimed his place after the lunch-time intermission, a general of the Alabama National Guard walked up to the auditorium doorway at 3:30 P.M. and spoke the most memorable words of the day: "It is my sad duty to ask you to step aside, on order of the president of the United States."

Governor Wallace exited. An armed guard atop the auditorium waved a flag. It was white, the color of surrender.

The last state in the union with an all-white university system had fallen. But in defeat, Wallace had scored a symbolic victory. The Kennedys had their representative Katzenbach confront Wallace alone, not wanting to expose James Hood and Vivian Malone to a personal

Students at a Birmingham high school, desegregated in the fall of 1963, express their approval of Governor George Wallace.

[87]

insult from their governor. But by allowing Wallace to take on the "central government," they had handed him an issue that would launch him into a national political orbit. Wallace made his first of several runs for president the following year. He rallied a large following nationwide behind the slogan of "states' rights"—which disguised racism as resentment against the U.S. government.

Meanwhile, by aligning his administration with the civil rights cause, John F. Kennedy had put his presidency on the line.

THE SECOND EMANCIPATION PROCLAMATION

*"[W]ho among us would be content to have the color
of his skin changed and stand in [the African American's] place?"*

—President John F. Kennedy, June 11, 1963

Only minutes before President Kennedy was to go on national television, the speech he was to deliver—one of the most important of his career—was still being written. But June 11, 1963, had been a busy day, what with Alabama governor George Wallace standing in the schoolhouse door down in Tuscaloosa.

Kennedy's approach to civil rights had undergone a big change in the weeks since Birmingham. If he continued to treat the "fires of frustration and

President Kennedy, right, confers with his brother Robert.

discord" flaring across the South as crises to be contained or snuffed out, almost all the administration's manpower would be spent dealing with civil rights. Kennedy was now proposing a radical solution, one that he was to announce on television that night: a federal law that would abolish segregation.

At 8 P.M. the cameras rolled. Kennedy's distinctive style was cool and dry, but tonight he spoke about the plight of African Americans with religious language and passionate conviction.

African-American demonstrators clash with police in Jackson, Mississippi, after a memorial march held for civil rights leader Medgar Evers, slain hours after President Kennedy's speech.

[89]

"We are confronted primarily with a moral issue," he said. "It is as old as the Scriptures and is as clear as the American Constitution." The president announced that he was introducing legislation that would ask Congress to "make a commitment it has not fully made in this century to the proposition that race has no place in American life or law."

Black people had a saying: "Free in '63." It meant that they would finally get their freedom 100 years after Abraham Lincoln liberated the Confederacy's slaves in 1863. On this night, Kennedy had issued a second Emancipation Proclamation, one that promised to finish the job Lincoln had begun.

Kennedy would be gunned down, as Lincoln had been, before he saw the end of segregation. But his law, passed as the Civil Rights Act of 1964, would be his shining legacy, and one of the great achievements of our democracy.

MEDGAR EVERS:
MARTYR TO MISSISSIPPI

In Jackson, Mississippi, Medgar Evers had watched President Kennedy announce his new civil rights bill on television with a new sense of hope. The NAACP's first full-time staff member in Mississippi, hired shortly after the *Brown* decision in 1954, Evers was "a lone wolf who traveled sort of lonely and dangerous trails," said a colleague. As a boy growing up poor on a farm, he had impressed his family as "the saint," because he was disciplined and clean-living.

Evers's main work for the NAACP was recruiting members (with difficulty) and investigating race crimes. In the late summer of 1955, he had donned overalls to interview black cotton pickers

Medgar Evers

Byron de la Beckwith, left, a fertilizer salesman from an old Mississippi family, later bragged about killing Medgar Evers. Two trials failed to end in a verdict. He was convicted of the murder in 1994.

about the murder of Emmett Till. Evers was targeted for harassment by the White Citizens Council and the police. To the crank callers who constantly threatened him, he replied, "Well, whenever my time comes, I'm ready."

Near midnight on June 11, 1963, Evers returned home after a long day's work. A White Citizens Council oddball named Byron de la Beckwith lay in wait for Evers behind a honeysuckle bush. He shot Evers in the back with a hunting rifle. Evers's last words, on the verge of the new world predicted hours earlier by Kennedy's civil rights address, were: "Turn me loose."

THE MARCH ON WASHINGTON

"Power is the active principle of only the organized *masses,
the masses united for a definite purpose."*

—A. Philip Randolph, labor leader

A. Philip Randolph

A. Philip Randolph, the Movement's gray wise man at 74, had seen it all. Since the 1920s, he had headed the Brotherhood of Sleeping Car Porters, the first major black labor union. (Sleeping car porters were men, almost always African-American, who attended to passengers in the overnight Pullman train cars.) Although Randolph was a Harlem magazine editor and socialist intellectual who had never worked the trains, he had turned his union base into the most dynamic civil rights alternative to the Talented Tenth elitism of the NAACP. "Power and pressure do not reside in few, an intelligentsia," Randolph said. "They lie in and flow from the masses." Indeed, one of his fondest disciples was E. D. Nixon, the sleeping car porter who had helped rally the masses of Montgomery behind their pathbreaking bus boycott.

Since late 1962, Randolph had been working on mobilizing African Americans behind the cause of economic opportunity. His project was a revival of a March on Washington he had

BAYARD RUSTIN: THE STRATEGIST

Bayard Rustin was the March's chief organizer and one of the Movement's most brilliant and prophetic idea men. Highly trained in Gandhian direct action, he had helped Philip Randolph put together the (canceled) 1941 March on Washington. One of Martin Luther King Jr.'s most influential advisers and the guiding force behind the creation of SCLC, Rustin had also taken part in the first freedom ride, the 1947 Journey of Reconciliation. Many segregationists had a field day with Rustin's open homosexuality and former Communist Party membership.

foreign aid—into jeopardy. Governors George Wallace of Alabama and Ross Barnett of Mississippi had testified before Congress that the "civil wrongs" bill was a Communist plot. Suddenly Randolph's march had become hugely important to the Kennedy administration as well as to the Movement. It had to strike the right balance of revolutionary push and mainstream acceptability.

organized in 1941 to protest racial discrimination in industries with government defense contracts during World War II. (He had called off the march after President Franklin D. Roosevelt agreed to create the Committee on Fair Employment Practice to bring justice to the workplace.) The sensational events in Birmingham lent fresh energy to Randolph's plans for a new march. Now its specific purpose would be to press for the passage of the Birmingham-inspired civil rights bill that President John F. Kennedy had introduced.

This proposed legislation was so controversial that it had thrown the Kennedy administration's other, unrelated programs—space, agriculture,

SHOWDOWN

On August 28, 1963, some 250,000 Americans, most of them black but many white, made their way to the nation's capital for the March on Washington for Jobs and Freedom. They flooded the mall in front of the Lincoln Memorial to hear speakers from all branches of the civil rights movement. There were performances by Mahalia Jackson, Joan Baez, Bob Dylan, and other singers, black and white. Hollywood sent ambassadors such as actors Marlon Brando and Burt Lancaster.

Just before the ceremony was to begin, the

A. Philip Randolph, front and center, and the NAACP's head,
Roy Wilkins, front and left, lead the March on Washington,
eight years to the day after the murder of Emmett Till.

angry words might set off a riot and wipe out all the gains of Birmingham. "I have waited 22 years for this," Philip Randolph pleaded with the SNCC hotbloods. In the end, the offending words were removed.

Randolph led the official remarks in his dignified baritone. A hush fell over the sun-soaked crowd when the NAACP's chief, Roy Wilkins, announced that 95-year-old W.E.B. Du Bois, the founder of the NAACP, had died on the eve of the March.

[93]

power struggle that had been simmering for the past three years between the young radicals in the Student Nonviolent Coordinating Committee (SNCC) and the Movement's older, more conservative leaders came to a boil. The issue was the speech that SNCC's chairman, John Lewis, planned to deliver. It included a threat that the Movement would "march through the heart of Dixie, the way Sherman did," referring to the Union general who had burned Atlanta.

The March's organizers were afraid that

A DREAM COME TRUE

It was the last speech of the day that resounded throughout history. Taking the podium at the Lincoln Memorial, Martin Luther King Jr. began to speak slowly, using bitter language: "There will be neither rest nor tranquility in America until the Negro is granted his citizenship rights. The whirlwinds of revolt will continue to shake the foundations of our nation until the bright day

MARIAN ANDERSON: FREEDOM SINGER

The second most memorable refrain in Martin Luther King Jr.'s "I Have a Dream" speech was the line taken from the song "America": "Let freedom ring." In a previous landmark performance at the Lincoln Memorial, on Easter Sunday of 1939, the world-famous black opera singer Marian Anderson had delivered those words after the Daughters of the American Revolution refused to let her sing in Constitution Hall, the auditorium the organization owned in Washington. After a public outcry, the concert took place nearby at the Lincoln Memorial, where Anderson was introduced by President Roosevelt's cabinet secretary Harold Ickes: "In this great auditorium under the sky, all of us are free." Nearly a quarter-century later at the March on Washington, she sang, "He's Got the Whole World in His Hands." Some wondered if she was referring to King.

of justice emerges." But King seemed to sense that his biting words were at odds with the joy welling through the crowd, as the black people of America staked such a peaceful claim on their nation.

He put aside his written text and returned to a rousing, melodic sermon he had given on several occasions, including a mass meeting during the Birmingham campaign. "I have a dream," was King's refrain. "I have a dream that my four little children will one day live in a nation where they will not be judged by the color of their skin but by the content of their character. I have a dream today!"

Never in the history of America had the dream of freedom seemed so close to fulfillment. The March on Washington affirmed the dramatic change in public opinion on civil rights. Those shocking images out of Birmingham, the dogs and fire hoses, were now countered by this splendid pageant of "black and white together," as the lyrics to "We Shall Overcome" predicted.

Symbolic triumphs of integration like the March on Washington can have a potent effect on the moral imagination of a nation. But reality inevitably intrudes on the dream. The children of Birmingham had one more tragic scene to play.

Martin Luther King Jr.: "Nineteen sixty-three is not an end, but a beginning. . . .
Again and again, we must rise to the majestic heights of meeting physical force with soul force."

THE CHURCH BOMBERS

[98]

The fatal bombing of the Sixteenth Street Baptist Church capped 16 years of nonfatal Klan dynamite attacks on black homes and churches in "Bombingham." The Ku Klux Klan had enjoyed the "friendship" of the Birmingham police, elected officials such as Bull Connor and Governor John Patterson, and the city's ruling industrialists. But as civil rights disturbances began to hurt the local economy, the Klan lost its powerful supporters. Days before the church bombing, five black children entered three previously white Birmingham schools under heavy police protection. The Klansmen struck back in lethal desperation over the end of "Our Way of Life."

The FBI identified five chief bombing suspects within weeks. All were veterans of Birmingham's violent Eastview 13 Klan, which had planned the beating of the Freedom Riders as well as at least one assassination attempt against civil rights leader Fred Shuttlesworth. The FBI's director, J. Edgar Hoover, refused to let the suspects stand trial at the time. He claimed that a southern jury would never convict on the available evidence (and was probably right).

The first Birmingham bombing suspect, Robert Chambliss, was prosecuted in 1977. Tommy Blanton and Bobby Cherry were convicted in 2001 and 2002. Two more suspects died without being charged.

ROBERT "DYNAMITE BOB" CHAMBLISS

A 59-year-old truck driver, Chambliss was the veteran Klansman behind the bombings of the late 1940s against black home buyers in a previously white neighborhood that became known as

Robert Chambliss

Dynamite Hill. He was considered city commissioner Bull Connor's "errand boy" within the Klan—which helps explain why Chambliss did not get caught. On the day before the church bombing, he boasted to his niece, "You just wait till after Sunday morning. They will beg us to let them segregate." Thanks in part to that niece's testimony, Chambliss was successfully prosecuted for first-degree murder in 1977 by Alabama Attorney General Bill Baxley. He died in prison in 1985.

THOMAS E. BLANTON JR.

The youngest of the church bombers at 25, Tommy Blanton was the son of a vicious and colorful Klan veteran known as "Pop." A Klan associate thought Blanton was not intelligent enough to make a bomb, but dumb enough to place it. His blue-and-white Chevrolet was spotted behind the Sixteenth Street Church at 2 A.M. on the morning of the bombing, the time that investigators believed that the bomb was planted. Blanton was convicted in 2001, after the discovery of an FBI tape recording of him in 1964 discussing the bombing with his wife.

Tommy Blanton

BOBBY FRANK "CHERRY BOMB" CHERRY

Cherry was a truck driver (and, like Chambliss, a wife beater and suspected child molester) who had been a member of the mob that attacked Fred Shuttlesworth in front of a local white high school in 1957. In

Bobby Cherry

the years after the bombing, Cherry told co-workers and relatives that he had helped "blow up a bunch of niggers back in Birmingham." Finally charged with the crime at age 69 in 2000, Cherry nearly escaped going to trial by pretending he had lost his mind. After psychiatrists ruled he was faking, Cherry was convicted of murder and imprisoned in 2002.

[99]

CHILDREN OF BIRMINGHAM

I was only a year younger than Denise McNair was at the time of the church bombing, yet the murder of the four girls had no impact on me. The color line had deprived me of the capacity to empathize with black children.

The general attitude of the white people in Birmingham toward the church bombing was that it had been done by "redneck" lunatics who were probably not even from our city. No one really drew a connection between our "nonviolent" bigotry and the Klan's dynamite. We saw the church bombing as a terrible thing that had befallen an otherwise upstanding, law-abiding community. Two months later, when President Kennedy was assassinated, white schoolchildren all over Birmingham cheered.

Denise McNair, 11

Carole Robertson, 14

Addie Mae Collins, 14

Cynthia Wesley, 14

THE BELOVED COMMUNITY

"I didn't expect to contribute a great deal, but I was going to be on the side of history that represented life instead of death."

—Anne Braden, white activist

At this point in the story, it might appear that there were no decent white people to be found in the South. In fact, many white Southerners knew that segregation was wrong but were afraid to say so. Their great fear was of one another: If they spoke out against segregation, their fellow whites might retaliate—either by hurting them physically or shunning them socially and economically.

The incredibly brave whites in the South who did work for the civil rights of African Americans were the charter members of Martin Luther King Jr.'s "beloved community." That was how he de-

Segregationists posted this misleading billboard throughout the South to discredit the civil rights movement.

scribed his vision of an integrated society whose best men and women— whites and blacks with "soul force"—struggled nonviolently against the enemies of progress and harmony.

What follows is a highly selective sample of the white people who took on the segregated South.

MYLES HORTON:
THE WIZARD OF HIGHLANDER

Myles Horton (in above photo, with hands clasped) returned home from theological school in New York in the 1930s to create the Highlander Folk

School in his native Tennessee. (The photo used in the billboard on page 101 was taken at the school's twenty-fifth anniversary celebration in 1957, attended by King.) A folk school is a sort of laboratory in which the disadvantaged and uneducated ("the folk") gather to work out solutions to their oppressed condition. During the 1930s and 1940s, Horton believed that the labor movement would be the savior of the region's poor and held workshops to train union organizers. In the 1950s, Highlander's focus shifted to civil rights. Among those who attended training sessions were Rosa Parks and E. D. Nixon (before the Montgomery bus boycott) and many of the militants of SNCC. Highlander was a bridge from the progressive struggles of the past to the modern civil rights movement. This was best symbolized by the catchy song Horton's wife, Zilphia, learned from striking tobacco workers in the 1940s and introduced to the Movement: "We Shall Overcome."

AUBREY WILLIAMS:
AMBASSADOR FROM THE NEW DEAL

Aubrey Williams, the poor son of an alcoholic Alabama blacksmith, had been one of the most exciting, racially liberal officials in President Franklin D. Roosevelt's New Deal and was one of Myles Horton's main comrades. It was Williams (wearing a bow tie in the billboard photo) who negotiated with Philip Randolph to cancel the 1941 March on Washington and persuaded Roosevelt to declare an end to discrimination in war industries. After returning to Alabama, Williams enlisted the liberal white holdovers from the New Deal behind the civil rights movement. The organization he headed, the Southern Conference Educational Fund (SCEF), was the only group actively trying to engage southern whites in the fight to end segregation. Southerners branded SCEF a "Communist front" and Highlander a "Communist training school."

ANNE BRADEN:
THE MOVEMENT'S POPULARIZER

Trained as a journalist, Louisville-based Anne McCarty Braden was one of the Movement's most effective publicity agents, able to get news coverage for endangered blacks like her close associate in Birmingham, Fred Shuttlesworth. In 1954, Braden and her husband and fellow

Anne Braden

journalist-activist, Carl, bought a house in a white Louisville neighborhood for a black family. It was promptly bombed. The authorities jailed Carl Braden rather than the bombers. The couple was hired by Aubrey Williams's Southern Conference Educational Fund to be SCEF's connection with the emerging civil rights movement. Anne served as sort of a den mother to the SNCC kids and recruited SNCC's first white staff member.

Lillian Smith

LILLIAN SMITH: WRITER ACTIVIST

Lillian Smith first scandalized her native South with her best-selling 1944 novel *Strange Fruit,* about an interracial love affair (and the lynching that ended it). In Georgia, she became a passionate advocate of civil rights, attacking segregation in her magazine, *South Today,* and in her memoir, *Killers of the Dream.* A longtime admirer of Gandhi and a member of the Congress of Racial Equality (CORE) since the 1940s, Smith became an outspoken supporter of Martin Luther King when he moved back to Atlanta. Smith criticized southern moderates for worrying more about the ugly results of segregation than about the evil of the institution. "It is the pus running out of the sore that offends them and not the sore itself," Smith wrote.

FRANK JOHNSON: JUDGE FOR JUSTICE

Frank Johnson was a country boy who, at age 37 in 1955, became the youngest federal judge in the nation. Most southern judges upheld segregation, but Johnson remained true to his rebellious roots as a native of an anti-Confederate North Alabama county whose young men fought in the Civil War on the side of the Union. Based in Montgomery, Johnson tackled the first of many civil rights cases in 1956: the desegregation of the city's buses during the boycott. Fellow white Alabamians threatened Johnson, his most colorful opponent being his old law school buddy, Governor George

Frank Johnson

Wallace. After Johnson scolded him for defying the federal government, Wallace blasted the judge as "an integrating, scalawagging, carpet-bagging, race-mixing baldfaced liar."

[103]

1964

COME...TOGETHER
Let Us Build A
Non-Violent World

MISSISSIPPI FREEDOM SUMMER

*"We must bring the reality of our situation to the nation.
Bring our blood to the White House door. If we die here, it's the whole society
which has pulled the trigger by its silence."*

—Prathia Hall, SNCC staff member, 1964

Bob Moses, center, with two co-workers in the Greenwood, Mississippi, SNCC office in March 1963. It was fire-bombed the next day.

Mississippi seemed immune to the historic changes brought about by Birmingham. President John F. Kennedy's segregation-ending bill, introduced after what he called "the events of Birmingham," would accomplish many momentous things once it was signed into law by President Lyndon B. Johnson as the Civil Rights Act of 1964. But it did not shield blacks against the racist violence that enforced segregation in places like Mississippi. Nor did it guarantee political opportunity: the black vote.

Without political muscle— the power to elect officials who might change the system—blacks had no chance of cracking open Mississippi's "closed society."

The Student Nonviolent Coordinating Committee (SNCC) had been working for years in Mississippi, "the middle of the iceberg," trying to register voters. "When you're not in Mississippi, it's not real," said the SNCC legend Bob Moses, "and when you're there the rest of the world isn't real." Moses, a quiet, dreamy, bespectacled 30-year-old intellectual, was a "Yankee," a product of New York's Harlem and the Harvard graduate school of philosophy. In 1960 he became the first Movement field worker to brave Mississippi.

Now it was 1964, and Moses knew that something had to give. The assassination of Medgar Evers had received publicity, if not justice. Most of the voting rights activists shot dead—Herbert Lee, Louis Allen, Clinton Walker—went to graves unmarked in the public conscience. But Moses had an idea about how to bring the national spotlight to darkest Mississippi: Freedom Summer.

Two African-American boys work in the Freedom Press Office in Hattiesburg, Mississippi, on the Mississippi Project, a campaign to increase black voter registration in the South.

The plan was for hundreds of white students from northern colleges to spend their summer break working on Moses's Mississippi Project. In addition to registering black voters for the fall presidential election, the college students would set up community centers to provide legal and medical services and teach children reading and math in "freedom schools."

Many inside SNCC objected to importing white Northerners. The group's focus had always been the long, hard haul of black community building. Freedom Summer sounded like a "traveling circus," the publicity-grabbing kind of stunt that SNCC had always criticized Martin Luther King Jr.'s Southern Christian Leadership Conference for—even when it worked, as it had in Birmingham. Since its founding, SNCC had had idealistic young white supporters, but some of the black staffers feared that the sophisticated, educated Yankees would intimidate illiterate Southerners, and might even try to take over SNCC itself.

Bob Moses overruled the objections. Everyone had begun to understand the way the system worked: Until some privileged white kids whose parents

THE CIVIL RIGHTS ACT OF 1964

Rammed through Congress by President Lyndon B. Johnson and signed into law on July 2, 1964, the bill created by the Kennedy administration would be the first meaningful civil rights legislation since Reconstruction. (There had been weak civil rights acts in 1957 and 1960.) Its most controversial feature, known as the "public accommodations section," removed the ugliest physical symbols of segregation, the white-only barriers against African Americans in restaurants, hotels, movie theaters, sports arenas, and other public facilities. The Civil Rights Act of 1964 also outlawed job discrimination on account of gender as well as race, religion, and national origin. The law gave the federal government the power to sue to desegregate schools.

Although white Southerners had predicted that blood would run in the streets if segregation was dismantled, the transformation was greeted rather peacefully, suggesting that the change was more cosmetic than radical. The events of Mississippi in 1964 showed how much work was still to be done.

President Johnson signs the Civil Rights Act of 1964 into law, with Martin Luther King Jr. looking on.

[107]

had wealth and connections put their lives on the line, no one was going to pay attention to any poor voteless black folk in Mississippi. "We know that the summer project was conceived with the idea of bloodshed," said one SNCC member. And the bloodshed was to be from whites.

SCHWERNER, CHANEY, AND GOODMAN

When Andy Goodman, a white college junior from New York, told his family he was going to Mississippi, he had explained, "This is the most important thing going on in the country. If someone says he cares about people, how can he not be concerned about this?" Goodman was among the first 250 Freedom Summer volunteers to go through orientation at a college in Ohio in June 1964 before heading south.

"I may be killed. You may be killed. The whole staff may go," the executive director of SNCC warned the volunteers. The State of Mississippi, meanwhile, prepared for yet another civil war, by acquiring 250 shotguns and an armored military vehicle. SNCC, too, had begun to disregard the "nonviolent" in its name and did not discourage black Mississippians from arming in self-defense.

Sunday, June 21, 1964, was Andy Goodman's second day in Mississippi. Goodman went out to a black community outside the little town of Philadelphia, with two seasoned civil rights workers, James Chaney, 21, a black Mississippian, and Mickey Schwerner, 24, a white New York social worker whose facial hair had earned him a nickname from the Ku Klux Klan: "Goatee." The Klan had burned a church in Philadelphia after its members reluctantly agreed to let it be used as a freedom school. Goodman, Chaney, and Schwerner wanted to lend their support.

As they were driving out of the community, the

[108]

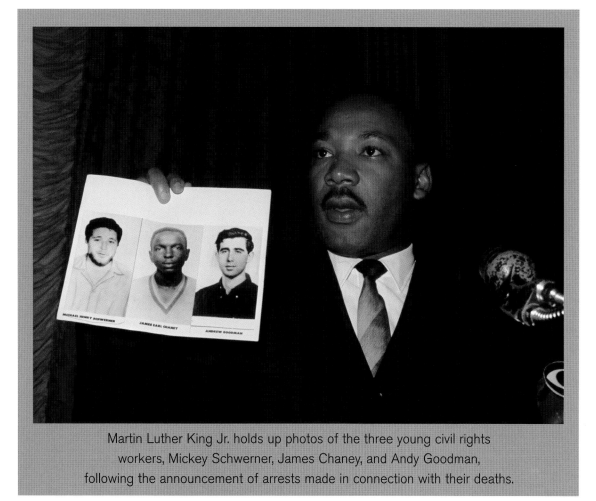

Martin Luther King Jr. holds up photos of the three young civil rights workers, Mickey Schwerner, James Chaney, and Andy Goodman, following the announcement of arrests made in connection with their deaths.

The burned station wagon of the three missing civil rights workers was located in a swampy area near Philadelphia, Mississippi.

county's chief deputy sheriff, Cecil Ray Price, picked them up on a fake traffic violation and took them to Philadelphia's tiny jail. Price held the three volunteers there till 10 P.M., then returned their driver's licenses and released them to the Klan. "They were nice to us, and we were nice to them," Price would tell one of the journalists who soon came to Philadelphia to look into the disappearance of Schwerner, Chaney, and Goodman.

Freedom Summer had barely begun, and already it seemed to have netted the predicted white victims. The worldwide publicity forced the federal government to intervene in Mis-

sissippi. President Lyndon Johnson personally ordered FBI director J. Edgar Hoover, who had shown no previous enthusiasm for protecting civil rights workers, to "put fifty, a hundred people after this Klan. . . . Now, I don't want these Klansmen to open their mouths without your knowing what they're saying." The hunt for the workers was still under way when Johnson signed the Civil Rights Act of 1964 on July 2.

Some Choctaws from the nearby Native American reservation had found the three young men's blue Ford station wagon smoldering next to a swamp. Finally, 44 days after they had vanished, paid informants within Philadelphia tipped off the FBI as to their whereabouts. Schwerner, Chaney, and Goodman were buried in a dirt dam on a local farm.

One of those on hand to shovel out the bodies was the deputy sheriff, Cecil Price. It was later discovered that Price had driven the civil rights workers from his jailhouse to the woods, where a squad of Ku Klux Klansmen had gunned them down. As one of the killers fired a bullet into Chaney's belly, he said, "Well, you didn't leave me nothing but a nigger, but at least I killed me a nigger."

[109]

The State of Mississippi never brought murder charges against the killers of the three young men. The U.S. Justice Department was able to get short prison sentences for Cecil Price, above, and six of the 19 men arrested for conspiring in the murders under a federal law passed during Reconstruction that made it a crime to deprive a person of his or her civil rights.

THE FREEDOM DEMOCRATIC PARTY

One of the major accomplishments of Freedom Summer was the formation of a political party to rival Mississippi's white-only state Democratic Party. (Because the Republicans had originally been the antislavery "Party of Lincoln," they had never had a following in the South.) The alternative, new Mississippi Freedom Democratic Party (MFDP) planned to send a delegation to the Democratic National Convention, where they were to officially nominate President Lyndon Johnson as their candidate in the November presidential election. As the August convention approached, the MFDP had 80,000 members, the vast majority of them black. The most celebrated of them was Fannie Lou Hamer. A barely literate, crippled, overweight, middle-aged sharecropper, who was the youngest of 20 children, Hamer was an inspiring example of how the Movement could motivate people without obvious resources to take charge of their destinies.

Hamer was among the MFDP's delegates to the Democratic convention in Atlantic City, New Jersey. It began on August 22, 1964, 18 days after the bodies of Schwerner, Chaney, and Goodman were found. The proceedings were dominated by the fight for recognition between Mississippi's white-only Democrats and the integrated MFDP challengers. Fannie Lou Hamer stunned a national television audience with her emotional plea to have her party recognized. "Is this America? The land of the free and the home of the brave?" Then she described being clubbed by whites in her native state—"I screamed to God in pain"— and began to cry in front of the cameras. Sitting next to her, waiting to be heard, was Mickey Schwerner's widow, Rita.

President Johnson was not pleased that this urgent democratic agenda was distracting the convention from the business of nominating him for president. He arranged to have the TV networks take Hamer off the air. Though Johnson's sympathies were with the civil rights movement, he knew that if he sided with the MFDP, he would offend southern white voters. So he maneuvered behind the scenes to make sure that the party "regulars"—Mississippi's white-only Democratic delegation—were seated instead of the MFDP.

This would prove to be the last time Mississippi sent an all-white delegation to a Democratic convention, but the idealistic MFDP organizers were shocked at being betrayed by a president they thought was the Movement's friend. The blow devastated some of SNCC's members, costing them their faith in the American system. In less than a year, Bob Moses resigned from SNCC and announced that he was changing his name to Bob Parris (his mother's birth name). "I will no longer speak to white people," he said. Eventually, Moses exiled himself to Africa.

Fannie Lou Hamer speaks at the Democratic National Convention.

[111]

After being elected by a landslide in November, Lyndon Johnson pledged to "eliminate every remaining obstacle to the right and the opportunity to vote" by passing the "goddamnedest toughest voting rights act."

To fulfill his vow that blacks would "see the Promised Land" during his presidency, Johnson sought the help of Martin Luther King. The Movement returned to Alabama for its last pure moment of glory: Selma.

SELMA

"Because it is not just Negroes, but really it is all of us, who must overcome the crippling legacy of bigotry and injustice."

—President Lyndon B. Johnson, March 15, 1965

State and local law-enforcement officers block civil rights marchers in Selma.

Sheyann Webb was all of eight years old and wasn't sure what "voting" meant. But that hadn't stopped her from joining the movement to register black voters in her hometown of Selma, Alabama. On her way to school one day, she had noticed the crowd of civil rights workers in front of Brown Chapel, which, to her amazement, included white people. Even though her parents told her to stay out of that Movement "mess," Sheyann soon became Martin Luther King Jr.'s "smallest freedom fighter." Whenever he came to Selma, he would hold her on his lap at the pulpit and let her lead her favorite freedom song, "Ain't Gonna Let Nobody Turn Me Around."

Like Sheyann, many of Selma's black adults did not understand what voting had to do with their lives. They didn't see that political power would enable them to have a say in who ran the town, the school board, and the police department. Voting was "white folks' business," and the white folks had taken pains to keep it that way in the Black Belt, the band of cotton-growing country that cut across the South and was named for the darkness of its rich soil as opposed to the skin color of its vast black majority. Because the white minority didn't want to be outnumbered at the polls, they had thought up ploys to keep blacks from voting. Besides the long-standing poll tax, which meant you had to pay to vote, there were limited registration days (two Mondays a month in Selma), difficult forms, and "good character" requirements—which one candid Alabama politician admitted would exclude Jesus Christ if he were voting the wrong way. If all else failed, a "citizenship" test made registrants answer questions such as "Who was President Zachary Taylor's vice president?" and "How many bubbles are there on a bar of soap?" In Selma, the capital of Alabama's Black Belt, only 325 of the 15,000 voting-age African Americans had been registered, compared with 9,300 of the 14,000 eligible whites. Somehow, barely literate whites always passed the tests, while black Ph.D.s failed.

SCLC held demonstrations in St. Augustine, Florida, in 1964 from March through June. Here, protesters "wade in" at a segregated beach on June 25, 1964. They were attacked by segregationists. A week earlier, during a "swim-in" at a motel pool, the owner poured skin-burning chemicals into the water. SCLC's St. Augustine campaign ended when President Johnson signed the Civil Rights Act of 1964 in July.

THE SHERIFF

Because the Civil Rights Act of 1964 had no strong provision to deal with voting discrimination, the Movement now turned its focus on the ballot. The Student Nonviolent Coordinating Committee (SNCC) had begun a big push in Selma following the Birmingham church bombing to try to channel grief and anger into constructive action. SNCC workers had been holding voter clinics and demonstrations at the courthouse, but had run up against the usual white wall of resistance. In late 1964, Amelia Boynton, a leading civil rights activist in Selma, asked Martin Luther King, who had just won the Nobel Peace Prize, to come help.

King's Southern Christian Leadership Conference (SCLC) had had workers in and out of Selma over the past year, but its main recent entanglement had been a thankless campaign to desegregate St. Augustine, Florida, the country's oldest city. That protest had yielded no solid victory, despite the excitement of "swim-ins" at segregated pools and violent Klan marches in retaliation.

Selma, Alabama, seemed the ideal spot for a confrontation. It could be the next Birmingham. The town even had a villain to rival Birmingham's Bull Connor. Selma's sheriff, Jim Clark, was a beefy, crude, and violent racist, with a scary equivalent to Connor's dogs and fire hoses: a posse on horseback.

More than ever, SCLC was handling its Selma project by catering to the media, the approach scorned by SNCC. King's "letter from a Selma jail" had been written before he was arrested on February 1, 1965, for leading 260 marchers to the courthouse to attempt to register. Four days later, the letter ("This is Selma, Alabama. There are more Negroes in jail with me than there are on the voting rolls.") appeared as a fundraising ad in the *New York Times*.

But even if SCLC was being a bit too strategic, Selma was also using King for his star quality and his access to national opinionmakers. This campaign was a case of the Selma community leading King rather than vice versa. The depth of the commitment in Selma had been signaled by a demonstration on January 22. More than 100 schoolteachers marched to the courthouse to protest Sheriff Clark's arrest of Amelia Boynton at a demonstration two days earlier. Sheyann Webb was amazed to see her teachers out there on the line. As a group, teachers had never been known as Movement boosters, partly because they answered to a white school superintendent.

[115]

BLOODY SUNDAY

It was a beautiful Sunday afternoon, and Lewis found himself at the head of a line of 600 marchers, sharing the leadership duties with SCLC's Reverend Hosea Williams. (King was in Atlanta.) Right up there in front with them was Sheyann Webb. A lot of people had told the girl she was too small, but she was so "spirited up" that she wasn't afraid. Singing freedom songs, the marchers walked east out of Selma, crossing the Alabama River on the Edmund Pettus Bridge. At

the highest point of the bridge, they looked down to the other side upon what Lewis described as "a sea of blue" uniformed state troopers, with tear gas masks dangling from their belts. Sheriff Clark's posse was among them, horses and all.

The major in command of the state troopers ordered the marchers to halt and go home. He gave them two minutes. Sheyann started to cry, and then obeyed the ministers' orders to kneel down and pray. The major issued the call: "Troopers, advance."

First came a line of uniformed cops, striding into the front row of marchers. John Lewis was eyeball-to-eyeball with one of the troopers, who then started clubbing him in the head. As Lewis buckled from a skull fracture, SCLC's Hosea Williams turned and ran. Canisters of tear gas were being hurled at the marchers, spewing a yellow fog. Then came the horses.

Sheyann ran as fast she could. The horses knocked some people off the bridge and down the riverbank. Hosea Williams picked Sheyann up. She told him to put her down because he was not running fast enough. The horses galloped

John Lewis, center, is downed by a state trooper's club.

after the fleeing marchers, their riders clubbing stragglers. Officers on foot shocked the demonstrators with cattle prods. Simply unable to believe the behavior of the white folks, Amelia Boynton, the godmother of the Selma campaign, turned to another woman and asked, "What do these people mean?" Then she was knocked unconscious by a trooper's billy club.

"Bloody Sunday" did not come to an end until Sheriff Clark's horses had chased the demonstrators all the way back to the steps of Brown Chapel. Cameras from the major television networks filmed the action. That night, ABC broke into its regular programming to air the blood-chilling news footage out of Selma. The ABC movie being interrupted was *Judgment at Nuremburg,* about Nazi Germany's crimes against humanity.

"WE SHALL OVERCOME"

At the urging of King, clergy and other interested citizens flocked to Selma from around the country. On Tuesday, March 9, King led 2,000 people over the Edmund Pettus Bridge. But because federal judge Frank Johnson had ordered that no march take place until he ruled on a related matter, King obeyed the troopers' order to stop. The marchers turned around and headed back to the church. SNCC workers, their resentment of SCLC breaking the surface, mockingly sang, "Ain't Gonna Let Nobody Turn Me Around." The anticlimactic sequel to Bloody Sunday became known as Turnaround Tuesday.

Still, that Tuesday ended in bloodshed. In the evening, a young white Unitarian minister from Boston named James Reeb left a black café with two other visiting white clergymen. A white local whacked him upside the head. After two days in a coma, Reeb died. As the country convulsed in protest over Reeb's death, some SNCC leaders compared that sorrowful reaction to the relative silence that had greeted the murder of the young black man, Jimmie Lee Jackson. They wondered if the Movement was accommodating the racism of a country that paid no attention to their struggle until it took the life of a white person.

On Monday, March 15, President Johnson went on national television and topped John F. Kennedy's modern Emancipation Proclamation of 1963. "It is wrong—deadly wrong—to deny any of your fellow Americans the right to vote in this country," Johnson said. With his hangdog glare, the president announced that he was sending voting rights legislation to Congress. He compared Selma to other landmarks of American

[119]

democracy such as Lexington, Concord, and Appomattox, where "history and fate meet at a single time in a single place to shape a turning point in man's unending search for freedom." In one of the most electric moments of his presidency, Johnson declared, drawing in his chin for emphasis, "And we shall overcome."

The SCLC ministers watching the address on TV that night began to cheer. C. T. Vivian stole a look at King and noticed a tear running down his cheek.

Martin Luther King Jr., center, former United Nations peacekeeping official Ralph Bunche, to the right of King, and John Lewis to the far left, lead the march to Montgomery on March 21, 1965. The leis were the gifts of a group of marchers from Hawaii.

ON TO MONTGOMERY

Judge Johnson lifted his ban on the Selma to Montgomery March. Governor Wallace claimed that he couldn't protect the "Communist-trained" troublemakers streaming into Alabama by the thousands. President Johnson federalized the Alabama National Guard and sent 2,000 additional soldiers to protect citizens exercising a constitutional right from their fellow Americans.

On Sunday, March 21, 4,000 people set out from Selma and headed east down the Jefferson Davis Highway on the 54-mile, five-day walk to Montgomery. The front of the march was a picture of melting-pot harmony: King, his fellow black Nobel Peace Prize winner Ralph Bunche, a rabbi, a priest, some nuns, a young white woman, and a white amputee on crutches, whom white Alabamians along the route ridiculed by chanting, "Left, left, left." Selma had become a magnet for celebrities, including actors Marlon Brando and Paul Newman. A number of the "marchers" just put in appearances on the route, driving off at night to a hotel bed.

A core group of 300 pitched tents in the fields, ate meals prepared back in Selma, and slept under the vigil of the U. S. military. The scene of Army helicopters hovering over the non-violent campsite was a mixed message of America's great strengths: democracy with the military might to back it up.

For the first three days, King was there for nearly every step of the way, even on Tuesday, when the marchers walked 11 miles in the rain and bedded down in mud. He ducked out to Cleveland for a fundraising speech on Wednesday. On Thursday, March 25, King was back in the lead, shaking off the reports of yet another plot against his life. More than 25,000 Americans, a thoroughly integrated crowd, rolled into the capital of Alabama that afternoon.

Taking a seat of honor on the speakers' platform near the statehouse was Rosa Parks. One could see King's first church, Dexter Avenue Baptist, close by. From the podium, King recalled

Marchers cross the Alabama River on the Edmund Pettus Bridge at Selma.

the distance they had traveled since their journey had begun with a bus boycott ten long years before. He quoted Mother Pollard, the ancient boycotter who had said, "My feets is tired but my soul is rested." There would be another "season of suffering," King predicted, but he left his audience with the sense that he himself was rested, on what would be the last major triumph of his career.

How long will it take to get freedom? King asked the crowd. "Not long," he said and summoned his genius at joining hope with reality: "because the arc of the moral universe is long, but it bends toward justice."

For her ninth birthday, Sheyann Webb asked her parents for a special present: She wanted them to become registered voters. They took Sheyann with them on their first trip to the polls. Her excitement turned to surprise when she saw

[121]

how simple the act of voting was. The only thing to it was marking a ballot with a check mark! All that struggling and suffering for something so basic to democracy, so fundamental to a human being.

VIOLA LIUZZO: FINAL MARTYR

In her quest to become a useful human being, Viola Liuzzo, 39, a white mother and part-time student from Detroit, had come down to Selma to work as a volunteer. On March 25, as she was driving a black protester back from Montgomery at the end of the Selma march, a carload of Ku Klux Klansmen overtook Liuzzo's green Oldsmobile near the Big Bear Swamp on Highway 80. They shot her fatally through the spinal cord.

One of those Klansmen was the FBI's paid informant, Gary Thomas Rowe. His co-conspirators would later claim that Rowe himself pulled the trigger. At the very least, this violent racist on the payroll of the U.S. government had done absolutely nothing to prevent Liuzzo's cold-blooded execution.

For a time, Rowe became a law-enforcement hero, testifying in court against his Klan brothers, who were nevertheless acquitted of the murder. But eventually, Rowe's troubling double life as an FBI informant, whose government status allowed him to go unpunished for the crimes he committed as a Klansman, became the subject of a congressional investigation. Rowe's career ended up as another black mark on J. Edgar Hoover's FBI.

As the Birmingham church bombing assured the passage of the Civil Rights Act of 1964, Liuzzo's death hastened the Voting Rights Act of 1965, which was signed by President Johnson on August 6, 1965. Along with the Civil Rights Act, the legislation would be the Movement's crowning achievement, giving African Americans a role in their own political future.

MALCOLM X

Malcolm X addresses a rally
in Harlem in May 1963.

The Movement was splitting apart. The sure sign came in Selma, Alabama. As the voting rights campaign there geared up for its Bloody Sunday milestone, one of the speakers who came to address the troops was Malcolm X. He was fierce, aggressive, anti-nonviolence, and not even Christian.

The Selma appearance was Malcolm X's first official contact with the civil rights movement. On February 4, 1965, soon after Martin Luther King Jr. had been jailed for marching in Selma, Malcolm appeared at Brown Chapel. He had been invited by the Student Nonviolent Coordinating Committee (SNCC). King's colleagues in the Southern Christian Leadership Conference (SCLC) were worried that Malcolm might whip up the crowd against the race he referred to as "white devils." Malcolm urged the packed chapel to take freedom "by any means necessary," his trademark slogan. His message seemed aimed as much at white America as at his black audience. "The white people should thank Dr. King for holding people in check," Malcolm told the Selma citizens, mentioning that other black leaders (and they knew who he meant) had no use for nonviolence.

Malcolm X had been a frightening and public reminder to whites of what a revolution *could* be like ever since he began criticizing King ("Reverend Dr. Chickenwing") in the days of the Montgomery bus boycott. To Malcolm, King was a "traitor to the Negro people" and nonviolence was a "wait-until-you-change-your-mind-and-then-let-me-up philosophy." Malcolm's comment on King's "children's miracle" in Birmingham was: "Real men don't put their children on the firing line." Malcolm's most scandalous comment was that the assassination of President John F. Kennedy had been a case of the "chickens coming home to roost," meaning Kennedy had gotten what he deserved.

A SEPARATE NATION

Malcolm X's background was the opposite of King's comfortable upbringing in the black middle class. He was born Malcolm Little in 1925 to followers of Marcus Garvey. His father died after being hit by a streetcar; his mother had a mental breakdown. Six-year-old Malcolm went to a foster home and later to reform school, in Michigan. When he was 16, he moved to Boston and

[124]

"BLACK"

Black Muslims used the word "black" to describe their race long before it became acceptable. They considered the popular polite term "Negro" ridiculous, as it was a Spanish word assigned to black people by Spanish and Portuguese slave traders.

Until 1966, African Americans considered "black" an insulting term. By embracing it, the Black Muslims were subtly rejecting the "color line" that divided even African Americans. As an old black folk song advised: "Now if you're white, you're all right. And if you're brown, stick around. But if you're black, get back."

became a drug dealer and burglar. At 21, he was in prison.

Encouraged by his brother, the jailed Malcolm joined the Nation of Islam, a small African-American religious sect based loosely on the Muslim faith. The religion had been founded during the Depression by a silk salesman (rumored to have been born in Arabia, though little is known about him) and was most popular among the southern immigrant population of northern cities. Its followers often abandoned the "slave name" of their ancestors and changed their last name to X (also the symbol illiterate people used instead of a signature).

The Black Muslims were nationalists and separatists. In contrast to integrationists like King, they urged blacks to behave as a separate nation unto themselves, responsible for their own betterment.

The Nation of Islam demanded that its followers, many of whom were from troubled backgrounds like Malcolm X's, observe strict discipline and morality. These requirements included a short haircut, avoidance of alcohol and tobacco, and a coat-and-tie uniform. The Nation was a masculine culture, aimed at restoring the confidence of the downtrodden black male. Its answer to white harassment was armed self-defense.

After leaving prison in 1952, Malcolm X became a prominent Black Muslim spokesman, a fiery orator and a brilliant debater. His fame grew not out of anything he did but out of his fearless expression of the pent-up rage that blacks had as a result of being discriminated against. "Most of us are attracted to things extreme," he explained, "primarily because of the extreme negative condition that we live in." Malcolm became a lecturer in great demand, though many blacks feared the trouble his words might provoke. But to the most hopeless, especially those in the North who were alienated from the black church, Malcolm was a thrilling example of manhood and racial pride.

Malcolm X speaks at Selma's Brown Chapel in February 1965.

[125]

MARCUS GARVEY: BACK TO AFRICA

Malcolm X was not the first proud black man to refer to the dominant race as "white devils." In the early 1920s, Marcus Garvey presided over a black nationalist movement far larger that anything the Nation of Islam would achieve.

In 1916, Garvey, a 29-year-old Jamaican journalist, dreamer, and spellbinding speaker, moved to New York and brought with him a two-year-old organization, the Universal Negro Improvement Association (UNIA). Preaching a message of extreme black pride—Africans were "the most moral people in the world"—Garvey became the first black leader to command a large mass following, mostly of solid working-class blacks. His goal was to give back the African continent, which was then under European rule, to its indigenous peoples and create a great black empire called the "United States of Africa." Although his ultimate hope was for African Americans to return to Africa, Garvey was for now content with the impressive black self-help empire he had built in the United States and the Caribbean: UNIA membership was conservatively estimated at 80,000, with 400 branches.

By 1920, Garvey's main focus had become his Black Star Line. This shipping company, which already owned three ships, would provide black people with first-class service around the Caribbean. The steamship line failed financially. In 1922 Garvey was criminally charged with using the mail to steal from his investors.

The UNIA came apart. Garvey's black nationalism curdled into a separatism so extreme that he entered into secret talks with the Ku Klux Klan (as would the Nation of Islam's Elijah Muhammad) and accused the NAACP's light-skinned leaders of using integration to "wipe out the Negro race."

In 1925 Garvey was sent to prison on the dubious mail-fraud charge. The government official who had pursued Garvey was an ambitious 24-year-old in the Bureau of Investigation named J. Edgar Hoover, who 35 years later dogged Martin Luther King.

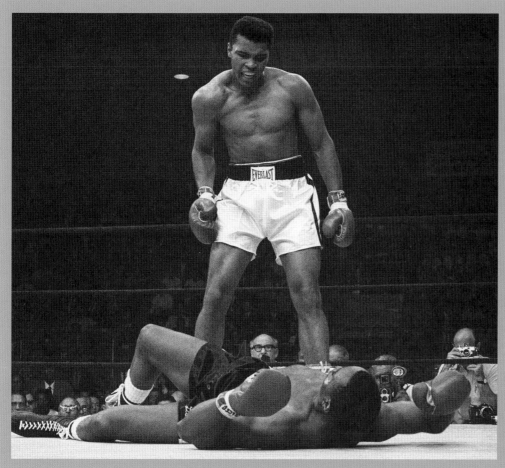

MUHAMMAD ALI: THE GREATEST

Cassius Marcellus Clay Jr. of Louisville, Kentucky, became the heavyweight boxing champion of the world in 1964 (he is pictured here knocking out Sonny Liston to defend the title). Two days later, he converted to the Nation of Islam under the influence of Malcolm X. Changing his name to Muhammad Ali, the fighter inflamed the anxieties of white America with assertions like "I am the greatest." As the in-your-face embodiment of black pride, Ali became a pop hero—the Beatles even came to visit him at his Miami gym. He offended the white mainstream when he refused to serve in the Vietnam War because of his religious beliefs. Ali was stripped of his title, and the government prosecuted him for draft dodging. Three years later, in 1971, the Supreme Court ruled that the government had acted improperly. He regained his title in 1974.

[127]

TRAITOR

Martin Luther King had been careful to keep Malcolm X at arm's length (although A. Philip Randolph was cordial). But in fact, by 1965, Malcolm's philosophy had grown closer to King's vision of a just, multiracial society. During a 1964 pilgrimage to the holy Muslim shrines in the Middle East, Malcolm met fellow Muslims of many different nationalities and began to recon-sider his anti-white stand. Back in Selma, Malcolm reassured King's wife, Coretta Scott King, that he had come to help her husband's mission.

Malcolm X's most urgent struggle was now with the top leader of the Nation of Islam, Elijah Muhammad, an uneducated but shrewd Georgia-born Chicagoan whose flock considered him a semi-divine "Messenger." After learning that

Martin Luther King Jr., left, and Malcolm X met only
this once, on March 26, 1964, in Washington, D.C.

Muhammad had fathered illegitimate children and then tried to smear their mothers' reputations, Malcolm withdrew from the Nation in 1964 to form his own Muslim group. Muhammad's followers condemned him as a traitor.

On February 21, 1965, less than three weeks after that historic appearance at the civil rights rally in Selma, 39-year-old Malcolm X gave another speech, before a Nation of Islam audience in New York. He was blasted by shotgun fire. The assassins were believed to be Black Muslims loyal to Elijah Muhammad.

In the end, Malcolm X had needed "armed self-defense" not against the "white devil," but against his own people. His influence, however, would reach well beyond the grave into the future of the Movement. The fury that Malcolm had unleashed in hard, glittering words soon materialized in real bodies on city streets across America.

WATTS

"Burn, baby, burn."

—Rioters in Los Angeles, California, August 1965

It was a "routine traffic stop." On the evening of August 11, 1965, in a rundown, garbage-littered black neighborhood near the Los Angeles airport, a white highway patrolman stopped a Buick driven by 21-year-old Marquette Frye, who had been drinking. Many people were out on the street trying to beat the heat. Frye's mother came out too, first to fuss at her son. But then her anger transferred to the patrolman. She jumped on the cop's back. The hurt and rage of a race, tamped down for decades if not centuries, suddenly burst out in this Los

A shoe store in Watts collapses in flames during the fourth day of rioting.

Angeles neighborhood soon to be famous worldwide as Watts.

In the year since the passage of the Civil Rights Act of 1964, African Americans were becoming aware of what that law abolishing segregation did not address: poverty, unemployment, and abuses by "The Man," the name blacks gave the overwhelmingly white police force where black despair collided most painfully with white power. These were the hardships, not segregated lunch counters and "WHITE ONLY" signs, felt by the black people of Los Angeles. As the white police chief summed up the situation: "We're on top and they are on the bottom."

On that hot August night in 1965, rumors circulated that the police had clubbed a pregnant black woman in the stomach or maybe they had choked a woman. A mob that grew to 2,000 people began throwing rocks and bottles at policemen and then stopping and overturning cars.

"HERE COME WHITEY"

In the morning came the first daylight attacks, against two white salesmen. A policeman shot and injured a young man looting a store. California's governor sent in National Guardsmen with bayonets ready. At 9:40 P.M. that Friday, a

A sign posted during the riots

Demonstrators push against a police car during the Watts riot.

sheriff's deputy was shot fatally in the stomach. He was apparently the first law-enforcement officer killed in a racial conflict over the ten years since the Movement emerged from the Montgomery bus boycott.

The *Los Angeles Times,* the leading newspaper in a city whose black population numbered 420,000, did not have a single African-American reporter. To get its front-page "Eyewitness Account" of the action, the editors had pulled Robert Richardson, a 24-year-old black messenger from the classified advertising department, and sent him out to the ghetto. The story he telephoned in to a white reporter would popularize two slogans for rioters of the future. "Here come Whitey, get him!" was one of the battle cries Richardson heard in Watts. The other was what the gangs of youths shouted after heaving their Molotov cocktails through storefronts: "Burn, baby, burn!"

When the Watts riot finally ended six days after Marquette Frye was pulled over, 34 people had been killed and 1,000 hurt, including 90 police officers and 136 firemen; 14,000 National Guardsmen had been ordered in; 4,000 adults and juveniles had been arrested; and an estimated $200 million worth of damage had been done to local property, including the community hospital where riot victims were being treated. More than a third of the 3,400 adults arrested had never been in trouble with the law before. That is why the Watts riot would be seen not as a crime spree of thugs and bad elements but as an uprising of ordinary citizens.

LOSS OF INNOCENCE

Watts was a turning point. Two years before, the first race riot of the civil rights era had occurred in Birmingham after Klansmen bombed the motel that had until recently been Martin Luther King Jr.'s headquarters. But that had been a mere preview. Some would argue that Watts was the worst race riot of the century.

The black people had lost their fear, and the freedom movement its innocence. Even though

Martin Luther King Jr., right, and Bayard Rustin, left, address a public gathering in Los Angeles. According to Rustin, Watts was "the first major rebellion of Negroes against their own masochism."

the great majority of those who died in the rioting were black, the feeling in the community was one not of sorrow but of pride. *Newsweek* reported, "The mood of Watts last week smacked less of defeat than of victory and power." When King toured the ruins, one of the locals yelled, "Go back where you came from."

The following year, riots rocked urban America. Forty-three cities in all, from Washington, D.C., to Chicago, to Cleveland, to Minneapolis, flickered with the fires of black rage, to the chants of "Burn, baby, burn." Within a year of his death, Malcolm X had been transformed from an extremist advocate of "any means necessary" into a prophet. King, meanwhile, reconsidered his dream: "I started seeing it turn into a nightmare."

[131]

1966

BLACK POWER AND THE MEREDITH MARCH

"Move on over or we'll move you out."

—Stokely Carmichael, SNCC chairman

James Meredith, the first black graduate of the University of Mississippi, looked every bit his strange self strolling down Mississippi's Highway 51 in combat head-gear and carrying an African walking stick. With his flair for independence and the courage that he thought of as "divine responsibility," Meredith had decided to make a solo "March Against Fear" to encourage African Americans to register to vote. He planned to walk 225 miles from Memphis, Tennessee, to Jackson, Mississippi, the capital of his native state.

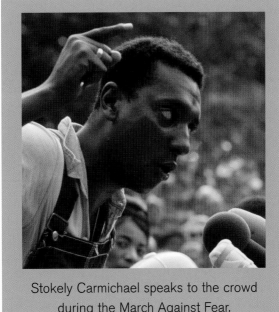

Stokely Carmichael speaks to the crowd during the March Against Fear.

On June 6, 1966, Meredith's second day out, an unemployed white man from Memphis fired a shotgun at him from a clump of honeysuckle and sent him skittering across the road. Martin Luther King Jr., along with representatives of the Student Nonviolent Coordinating Committee (SNCC) and the Congress of Racial Equality (CORE), hurried to Meredith's hospital bedside. Although the major civil rights figures had originally seen Meredith's lonely trek as a sort of crackpot gesture, they now vowed to continue the protest. It was the first spectacular

James Meredith pulls himself across Highway 51 after being shot.

group effort since the 1965 Selma to Montgomery March. By the time it was over, the modern civil rights movement would be in disarray.

"WHAT DO WE WANT?"

The youngest leader of the Meredith March was 25-year-old Stokely Carmichael, a hard-charging Howard University graduate, so confident that, as one writer put it, he could "stroll through Dixie in broad daylight using the Confederate flag for a handkerchief." The month before, in a bitter battle over the soul of SNCC, Carmichael had become the organization's new chairman, replacing John Lewis, hero of the Freedom Rides and Selma. Lewis had tried in vain to keep SNCC committed to the peaceful vision of justice that King referred to as the "beloved community." Carmichael, born in Trinidad and raised in New York, represented the forces of militant separatism who wanted to abandon nonviolence and kick out SNCC's white staff members.

On the Meredith March, Carmichael decided to take full advantage of the spotlight that inevitably followed King. He picked his moment to unveil SNCC's angry new direction. Along the march's route in the Mississippi town of

Greenwood, Carmichael was jailed for pitching tents for the protesters in a black playground. When he was released, he addressed a night rally of 3,000. "Everybody owns our neighborhoods except us . . . ," Carmichael said. "Now we're going to get something and we're going to get some representing. We ain't going to worry about whether it's white—maybe black. Don't be ashamed. We. Want. Black. Power!"

Movement speakers often engaged in a back-and-forth with their audience, and the answer to "What do we want?" would always come back, "Freedom now!" Carmichael coached this audience to give him a different response, a new slogan that would shock most of the Movement as well as white America. "What do we want?" he said, "Black Power!" Soon the responses of "Black Power!" were loud and, to many uttering them, shockingly brave.

ON OUR OWN

"Black Power!" was the new catchphrase of civil rights, though no one was saying whether it meant political power, economic power, or the brute power of armed force. Whatever it was, the Movement's old nonviolent warriors were out-

raged. Roy Wilkins, the head of the NAACP, felt that it meant "anti–white power" and called it "the father of hatred and the mother of violence." The March on Washington's mastermind, A. Philip Randolph, said it was a "menace to racial peace and prosperity." The Movement's white supporters backed away, and its enemies predicted a race war. SNCC basked in its isolation: "What we do from now on," said one staff member, "we will do on our own."

To Martin Luther King, Black Power was a way to turn a color that had once meant shame and inferiority into one of pride and challenge. As the preferred word for African American, *black* now replaced *colored* and *Negro,* putting the race on the same level as "white." But King recognized that Black Power would not fulfill the dream of freedom. "If you really have power," he said, "you don't need a slogan."

Black Power was heading toward an exaggerated aggressiveness that was largely symbolic. But King's nonviolence was no longer the answer either. Having achieved its major victories in the South, his movement was meeting its match up north, in Illinois, a state that called itself the Land of Lincoln.

[135]

CHICAGO

"I have never seen such hate, not in Mississippi or Alabama, as I see here in Chicago."

—Martin Luther King Jr., 1966

The American Nazi Party marches across from the church where Martin Luther King Jr. announces more demonstrations in Chicago's white neighborhoods in 1966.

[136]

Martin Luther King Jr. had always stressed that racism was an American problem, not a southern exception. When Alabama's "Segregation forever!" governor George Wallace made a limited run for president in 1964, he won an astounding one-third of the vote in the northern states of Indiana and Wisconsin. By 1966, even among white supporters of civil rights, there was a backlash against the Movement. This may have been because of Black Power or because, as King suggested, African Americans were now daring to challenge the white folks' "financial privilege."

The culture of black hopelessness that had led to the explosion in Los Angeles's Watts neighborhood convinced King that it was time to take the Movement north. The first target of his Southern Christian Leadership Conference (SCLC) outside the South was Chicago, Illinois.

In 1966, the Midwest's "City with Big Shoulders" was still one of the most segregated places in the country. As the most popular destination of the Great Migration of southern blacks from field to factory over the previous decades, Chicago had a huge African-American population of one million, a quarter of the city's residents. A conspiracy of real-estate agents, politicians, and businesses had made it nearly impossible for blacks to buy or rent housing in white neighborhoods. Those who tried often saw their new homes bombed or burned down. As a result, African Americans had been confined to large slums, paying high rents for awful living spaces and poor services. It was these discriminatory housing patterns that SCLC decided to take on, calling Chicago "the Birmingham of the North."

STRIKING OUT

Even before confronting the white-only neighborhoods of Chicago, SCLC's staff—including the one-of-a-kind James Bevel and a future presidential candidate named Jesse Jackson—had to adjust to a black population much different from the southern folk they were used to. In the North, the black church, the engine of the Movement, was not as influential as it was down south. And in contrast to the children who pulled off the sweet victory of Birmingham, the youth culture of Chicago's slums was dominated by

street gangs. Nonviolence was difficult to sell. As King's best friend, Ralph Abernathy, summed it up, "these young hard-eyed black boys had no respect for anything or anybody. To them a preacher was the next worse thing to a policeman, and religion was for old folks and suckers."

In July 1966, a riot broke out after policemen arrested black youths for turning on fire hydrants to cool themselves in the scorching summer heat. King, who had taken up residence in a slum apartment for the campaign, tried to calm down the angry young rioters. He was unable to reach his audience. The Chicago rioting continued for two days. It had spread over 600 blocks and resulted in two deaths by the time the National Guard was called in. Many white people held King responsible. The *Chicago Tribune* called him and SCLC "paid professional agitators."

King was beginning to conclude that every white person was, at best, "unconsciously a racist." And many Northerners were consciously, viciously so. When King began staging marches in all-white neighborhoods, the residents rioted. On August 5, 1966, a mob of more than 4,000 whites hurled bottles, eggs, and cherry bombs at King and his 800 marchers, despite the presence

[137]

Martin Luther King Jr. ducks after being hit on the head by a rock during a protest in August.

[138]

of 1,000 policemen. A rock hit King in the head, knocking him to his knees.

DOUBLE CROSS

As rioting on both sides threatened to turn into all-out bloodshed, Chicago's longtime boss, Mayor Richard Daley, agreed to negotiate with King. In the resulting "Summit Agreement," Daley promised the Movement everything and then delivered nothing. King and SCLC seemed to have forgotten the lesson of Birmingham: Target the economic interests, not the elected officials—unless you've got enough votes to make the politicians listen.

The real-estate firms for which Mayor Daley spoke paid no attention to his agreement and went right on denying housing to blacks. But the double-crossers who stunned King the most were Chicago's powerful blacks who were in Daley's hip pocket. Some of them had marched with King in Selma. Back on their own turf, they were working actively to get SCLC out of town, willing to crush the interests of their own people to safeguard their personal power.

SCLC left Chicago in shock. White Americans were offended by racist brutalities as long as they had occurred down south. In the North, however, whites put the blame on the activists for provoking the violence. A civil rights bill before Congress that year was all set to outlaw discrimination in housing, the issue at the heart of King's Chicago campaign. With the Movement's moral authority slipping, the bill did not pass, reversing the momentum of a decade.

THE BLACK PANTHERS

"[If] you drive a panther into a corner, if he can't go left and he can't go right, then he will tend to come out of that corner to wipe out or stop its aggressor."

—Bobby Seale, co-founder of the Black Panthers

Black Panther chairman Bobby Seale, left, wearing a Colt .45, and Huey Newton, defense minister, with a shotgun

Having invented the slogan "Black Power," the Student Nonviolent Coordinating Committee (SNCC) could find no winning way to turn it into action. The most visible agents of Black Power were a SNCC spin-off named after the black panther, the symbol for an all-black political party that SNCC's Stokely Carmichael had organized in rural Alabama in 1965.

Founded in Oakland, California, in October 1966, the Black Panther Party for Self-Defense seemed to be more effective at theater than at the revolution proposed in the group's "Ten Point Program," which included demands for land, bread, housing, education, clothing, justice, and peace. Although the Panthers attracted talented members and did some constructive community organizing (they ran a breakfast program for poor children), the white media paid more attention to their black leather jackets and berets, their photogenic poses, and their shock tactics. In May 1967, 30 Panthers marched into the California state capitol carrying guns to dramatize their favorite cause: the right to bear

Black Panthers argue with a California state policeman at the capitol in Sacramento after he disarmed them on May 2, 1967.

Eldridge Cleaver was the Panthers' minister of information and was credited with the much-quoted line: "You're either part of the solution or part of the problem." In 1968, he published a widely read book, *Soul on Ice*, written while he was in prison for assault.

arms in self-defense against the police, or "pigs."

The Panthers' founders were Huey Newton, a nighttime law school student, and Bobby Seale, who had worked as a jazz drummer, comedian, and metal worker. The two became celebrities and heroes to black youth and to suburban white kids, much like hip-hop artists are today. Newton was charged with killing an officer during a shoot-out between the Panthers and the police in October 1967. (His conviction for voluntary manslaughter was subsequently overturned.) "Free Huey!" became a rallying cry among 1960s youth—as did the Panthers' proposal: "Off (kill) the pigs." Stokely Carmichael left SNCC to become the Panthers' honorary prime minister in 1967, but the group's acceptance of white radicals went against his strict separatism.

SETTLING FOR FEAR

Although the Panthers were singled out for severe abuse by the police and the FBI, they themselves indulged in crime that could not be called "political," such as drug dealing, burglary, assault and battery, and murder. The Panther membership included many women who did the hard daily work. But some men used their exag-

SNCC's H. Rap Brown is handcuffed and arrested in 1967 on charges of inciting a riot in Cambridge, Maryland. In 2002, he was sentenced to life imprisonment for killing a sheriff's deputy in Atlanta during a 2000 shoot-out.

gerated masculinity as an excuse to indulge in violence, even against females.

The Black Panthers were influential in their day, inspiring militant organizations among Puerto Ricans, Mexican Americans, and Native Americans. Hungry for dignity in a society that did not want them to step out of their place, more blacks had decided that if they couldn't get whites' respect, they would settle for fear.

In the summer of 1967, the Watts disaster was replayed on an even deadlier scale in Detroit, Michigan, and Newark, New Jersey. Riots were replacing demonstrations. The country's attention had turned to the bloody war in Vietnam. SNCC, once the great hope of the "beloved community," was now chaired by H. Rap Brown, an activist who would serve time for armed robbery. Brown offered a lasting insight into the soul of America: "Violence is necessary. It is as American as cherry pie."

1968

MEMPHIS

"I may be crucified for my beliefs, and if I am, you can say, 'He died to make men free.'"

—Martin Luther King Jr.

National Guardsmen display their bayonets as striking sanitation workers and their supporters march in Memphis.

Martin Luther King Jr.'s four young children hadn't seen much of their father in the early months of 1968. He had been busy planning the most ambitious project of his career: the Poor People's Campaign, a mass camp-out of thousands of poor Americans in Washington, D.C. Toward the end of March, his wife, Coretta, suggested that he take their two sons along on his speaking tour to round up participants for the new protest. After a day of nonstop rallies in rural Georgia, they returned home to Atlanta way past midnight. It was clear that King's greatness was beyond the grasp of seven-year-old Dexter. "You know, Mommy," he reported to Coretta, practically sleep-walking, "I don't see how my daddy can do so much and talk to so many people and not even get tired at all!"

The world had changed a lot since the birth of the Kings' first child, Yolanda (Yoki), three weeks before Rosa Parks refused to give up her seat on a bus. King and his Movement had accomplished an astounding amount. By creating a new form of revolutionary

Ralph Abernathy, right, and Martin Luther King Jr., center, lead the March 28 march in Memphis.

[144]

protest in America, they had brought about the end of legal segregation through the Civil Rights Act of 1964 and had extended political power to African Americans through the Voting Rights Act of 1965. But since the victorious Selma to Montgomery March, even black journalists had begun to pronounce King's strategy of nonviolent demonstrations "old hat." King was stuck between an increasingly militant segment of blacks who considered him conservative ("old" at 39) and

sympathizers for whom he had grown too radical. In 1967, for the first time in a decade, Martin Luther King had failed to make the Gallup Poll of the ten most admired Americans.

The civil rights movement had been pushed out of the headlines by another conflict dividing the country: the unwinnable war on the other side of the world in Vietnam. Its supporters believed that America was taking an essential stand in Vietnam to prevent the spread of Communism. But an antiwar movement was gaining momentum, and one of King's most talented staffers, James Bevel, had gone to its ranks. After much soul-searching, King had come out squarely against the war in 1967, calling racism, poverty, and war "the triplets of social misery." By opposing the Vietnam War, he made an enemy of the man waging it, President Lyndon B. Johnson. The Movement then lost its most powerful ally. (Johnson had appointed the former NAACP lawyer Thurgood Marshall to the Supreme Court in 1967, making him the first black justice.)

Throughout King's career, the Movement had always operated on the belief that progress was possible if the federal government was on your side. But now King was beginning to think that government was part of the problem. White European immigrants, he pointed out, had received plenty of help from the state—public universities, low-interest loans, and farming aid. As for the government's attitude toward blacks: "You set him free," he said of the Emancipation Proclamation, "but you didn't give him bus fare to the city." King called for a radical restructuring of the society, a "redistribution of the wealth," to balance the extremes of rich and poor. Such language struck some as "un-American."

GARBAGE MEN

The Poor People's Campaign, scheduled for the spring of 1968, reflected the change in King's thinking: It wasn't just black people whose rights he was fighting for; it was poor people of all colors. "This is not a race war," he said, "it is now a class war." So citizens representing all colors and ethnic backgrounds, Latinos and Native Americans as well as African Americans, would take up residence in the tent village that SCLC was building right in the nation's capital.

While trying to pull the Poor People's Campaign together, King received a call from James Lawson, an SCLC colleague in Memphis, Tennessee. Garbage collectors on strike there desperately needed his presence. The black community had mobilized behind the 1,300 striking sanitation workers, holding mass meetings and daily marches—somber, dignified demonstrations with pickets bearing a simple message: I AM A MAN.

King's aides advised him against getting involved. Planning and financing a project as controversial and mammoth as the Poor People's Campaign was already challenging SCLC's famously disorganized staff. (Among the creative protests being considered were sick people filling hospital waiting rooms and needy people visiting their congressmen and senators.) But the Memphis strike was a cause King could not resist. The sanitation workers, who were nearly 100 percent African-American, were the perfect example of the intersection between race and class. They were among the lowliest, worst-paid laborers in all of society, humans treated like the garbage they handled. "Memphis," King said, "is the Poor People's Campaign in miniature."

On March 18, 1968, King made a hugely successful appearance before a Memphis audience of 15,000. He returned ten days later to lead a

[145]

The teens' violence at the March 28 march had been encouraged by a militant youth organization called the Invaders. They felt ignored by the older, more established civil rights leaders and wanted to embarrass them and scare the white people at the same time.

his hotel. By the end of the day, a black teenager was dead, and 62 people were hurt, some by gunfire. Thirty-eight hundred National Guardsmen had been rushed in.

King was badly shaken. This was the first march in which black people under his leadership had become violent. He began to have aching doubts about the Poor People's Campaign, about whether he could maintain nonviolence among the tens of thousands of discontented souls scheduled to camp out in Washington within weeks. He wondered if nonviolence was even possible anymore as a revolutionary strategy. The press was bashing him, blaming him again for the bloodshed. King considered canceling the Washington campaign. But then he decided he would go back to Memphis to make things right. From there he would proceed to the nation's capital with his army of poor people.

TO THE MOUNTAINTOP

On April 3, 1968, the Memphis-bound plane from Atlanta was delayed by a bomb threat. The pilot

mass march through downtown. Flying in from New York at the last minute, King was hustled to the front of a crowd of 6,000 people. As they set off on their march, a well-coordinated group of young black men began smashing glass storefronts and looting merchandise. The police fired tear gas. Amid the roaring chaos, aides whisked King down a side street and off to the safety of

explained to the passengers, "Dr. Martin Luther King is on board." King had lived so long under the threat of murder that he claimed, "If there is any one fear I have conquered, it is the fear of death." But recently, Coretta Scott King had noticed in her husband "a sense of fate closing in." After arriving that night in Memphis, amid a terrible rainstorm, King told the mass meeting of the pilot's comment about the bomb. His eyes welled with tears as he continued:

"Well, I don't know what will happen now. We've got some difficult days ahead. But it really doesn't matter with me now, because I've been to the mountaintop. And I don't mind. Like anybody, I would like to live a long life; longevity has its place. But I'm not concerned about that now. I just want to do God's will. And he's allowed me to go up to the mountain. And I've looked over. And I've seen the Promised Land. I may not get there with you, but I want you to know tonight that we, as a people, will get to the Promised Land. So I'm happy tonight. I'm not worried about anything. I'm not fearing

any man." And then he quoted the lines from the "Battle Hymn of the Republic" with which he had joyously concluded the Selma to Montgomery March three years earlier: "Mine eyes have seen the glory of the coming of the Lord."

On the next day, April 4, hope returned to King and his SCLC colleagues. It was, after all, the Easter season, the time of year when they had resurrected the civil rights movement in Birmingham five years earlier. A Memphis judge had just given a green light to the big march

Martin Luther King Jr. in Memphis, April 3, 1968: "I may not get there with you."

THE FBI VERSUS MARTIN LUTHER KING

The Federal Bureau of Investigation had been out to get Martin Luther King since 1961 for a complex variety of reasons. One of them was that the FBI's director, J. Edgar Hoover, was a racist. Another of Hoover's motives in trying to ruin King was to hold on to the enormous power he had built up over five decades.

Hoover had made his name chasing down Communists in this country. By the time King burst onto the scene, the American Communist Party had dwindled to practically nothing. But if Hoover could tie the great new civil rights revolution to Communism, he would revive the threat that had kept him in power all those years and have the added satisfaction of stopping the Movement.

During the Kennedy administration, FBI agents investigated King and found no evidence of Communist influence on the civil rights movement. But because one of King's aides and an unpaid white adviser had once belonged to the Communist Party, Hoover was able to get clearance to spy on King and his associates through telephone wiretaps. The most damaging information the wiretaps turned up was that King was unfaithful to his wife.

This discovery shifted Hoover's focus from proving that King was a Communist to exposing him as an "evil, abnormal beast." (Hoover gathered details on the sex lives of many public figures, including the Kennedys.) When King won the Nobel Peace Prize in 1964, the FBI sent tapes supposedly recording King's extramarital activities to various newspapers as well as to King's wife, Coretta, with a note urging him to commit suicide.

When news organizations refused to print the FBI's leaks, Hoover switched strategies again. This time, the FBI's Counterintelligence Program (known as COINTELPRO) disrupted SCLC's operations through a variety of tricks. FBI agents tried to derail the Poor People's Campaign by spreading rumors that participants would have their names taken and lose their welfare checks.

For years, many people, including members of King's family and SCLC's staff, believed that the FBI had been somehow involved in King's assassination.

MO. DEPT. OF CORRECTIONS
00416

James Earl Ray

Conspiracy theories have haunted this case. James Earl Ray, a white petty criminal, was convicted of murdering King with a hunting rifle fired from the bathroom window of a boardinghouse. Many people have found it hard to believe that Ray could have acted alone. In recent years, King's family members announced their certainty that Ray was innocent. He died in 1998 while serving a life sentence.

SCLC had scheduled for the next day, to redeem the violence of March 28. Andrew Young, one of King's top aides, had done most of the testifying for SCLC. A dentist's son from New Orleans, Young was so smooth with white folks that his SCLC colleagues teasingly called him "Uncle Tom." He came into King's room at the Lorraine Motel to deliver the good news. King was so delighted with the court decision that he started a pillow fight. The other officers of SCLC joined in. The horseplay did not end until the Movement's high command lay stacked on top of one another on the motel bed.

ALL OVER

In Atlanta, Coretta Scott King was taking her daughter Yoki shopping for an Easter dress. Martin Luther King treated the season as a time of material sacrifice, as when everyone wore denim to church on Easter in Birmingham back in 1963. But Coretta had decided that was too much virtue to lay on a fashion-conscious 12-year-old. Yoki got her Easter finery.

It was close to suppertime when Coretta and Yoki King got home. In Memphis, King and his staff were about to pile into a white Cadillac, courtesy of a local funeral home, to go have din-

[149]

Martin Luther King Jr. lies shot while his companions point to where the gunfire originated.

ner with one of their local hosts. King loved soul food so much that he had made his friend Ralph Abernathy call to find out what was on the menu—candied yams, pig's feet, and chitlins, it turned out.

Moments past 6 P.M. on April 4, 1968, King went out on the balcony of the Lorraine Motel. He called down to Jesse Jackson, one of the newer additions to the SCLC staff, and invited him to join them for dinner. They had had a falling-out earlier that spring over Jackson's opposition to the Poor People's Campaign. King had accused

his young, ambitious lieutenant of being out only for himself. But now all seemed forgiven.

King decided he needed to go back into his room to get a jacket. Before he reached the door, there was a popping sound, like a car backfiring. King collapsed on the Lorraine Motel's concrete balcony. He had been shot through the right cheek.

Ralph Abernathy rushed out of his room and cradled his best friend in his arms. Andrew Young knelt beside him and sobbed, "Oh, my God, my God, it's all over."

THE POOR PEOPLE'S CAMPAIGN

Four weeks after King's assassination, in the wake of widespread riots mourning the death of nonviolence, SCLC went ahead and built its "Resurrection City" shantytown in the capital, where former SNCC chairman Stokely Carmichael had recently urged rioting blacks, "Get you your gun." In May, as many as 2,500 poor people, including some white folks, filled the tents and sheds. But the Poor People's Campaign ended up being a disaster. Rains turned the village to muck. Youth gangs harassed the protesters. Fights broke out.

It had been a long year since Robert Kennedy, now a senator from New York, provided the flash of inspiration that had become this disappointing finale to Martin Luther King's career. "Tell him to bring the poor people to Washington," he had advised a young NAACP lawyer in 1967 before she was to meet with King.

An estimated 59,000 attend the Poor People's "Solidarity Day" rally.

Three weeks after the first tenants moved into Resurrection City, Kennedy—a strong civil rights supporter hoping to succeed his brother as president—won California's critical Democratic primary for the presidential nomination. Making his victory speech in Los Angeles, he was shot dead. When President Kennedy was killed, Robert Kennedy had said, "An assassin never changed the course of history." But 1968 proved him wrong.

[151]

THE UNFINISHED WORK

"The destiny of the colored American . . . . is the destiny of America."
—Frederick Douglass, 1862

Only under rare circumstances, like war, do individuals realize with certainty that what they are taking part in is History. The civil rights struggle, America's second Civil War, was one of those extraordinary phenomena. War touches its participants profoundly. It can strengthen them to face life's future battles, or it can turn them into peacetime casualties, who either abandon the good fight or seek to re-create it in unconstructive ways. And so the civil rights movement has left an interesting range of legacies.

Four years after feeling that the world had come to an end, Andrew Young left the Southern Christian Leadership Conference (SCLC) to become the first African American elected to Congress from Georgia since Reconstruction. Young went on to serve as President Jimmy Carter's ambassador to the United Nations and, from 1982 to 1990, as mayor of Atlanta.

John Lewis, the hero of the Freedom Rides and heart of the Student Nonviolent Coordinating Committee (SNCC), continued to pursue Martin Luther King Jr.'s dream of the "beloved community" and was included in a 1975 *Time* cover story on "Saints Among Us." Since 1986, he has served a racially mixed district of Atlanta in the United States House of Representatives, rising to become one of Congress's most respected members.

Another SNCC hero, Bob Moses, became so upset over the Vietnam War that he moved to Africa and lived in Tanzania until 1976. In the 1990s, he resumed his civil rights work in Mississippi from an unlikely angle: math. Moses taught poor blacks first-year algebra as the modern means of self-empowerment, which he considered the equivalent of the 1960s' right to vote.

Many Movement stars had a hard time coming off what was known as "freedom high" and adjusting to ordinary life. Stokely Carmichael, the Black Power militant who ousted Lewis as SNCC's chairman in 1966, ended up exiling himself to Guinea, in Africa, and taking the African name Kwame Ture. For 20 years he answered his phone, "Ready for the revolution!" He died of cancer at age 57 in 1998. His fellow Black Power celebrity, Huey Newton, was shot dead in 1989 by a crack dealer he had refused to pay, in a rough Oakland, California, neighborhood where he had once recruited for the Black Panther Party.

The most puzzling post-Movement career belonged to James Meredith, the first black graduate of the University of Mississippi. Undeniably brilliant, Meredith earned a law degree from Columbia University and then had an erratic career path. In 1989, having decided that white liberals were his race's "greatest enemy," he joined the staff of the arch-conservative senator Jesse Helms of North Carolina and two years later campaigned for David Duke, a neo-Nazi and former chieftain of the Ku Klux Klan, in Duke's unsuccessful bid to be governor of Louisiana.

Author Diane McWhorter with Fred Shuttlesworth. In 2004, he became acting president of SCLC, succeeding Martin Luther King III.

[153]

Perhaps the Movement veteran who came closest to Martin Luther King's model of charismatic, integrationist leadership was Jesse Jackson. Besides his impressive runs for president, Jackson worked to "democratize" capitalism by creating progressive partnerships between private businesses and government. But Jackson (whose son is now a Congressman from Chicago) could not shake his image as an opportunist, dating back to King's assassination: He had gone on TV the next day wearing a stained shirt he was said to have dipped in King's blood.

Linda Brown, whose last name rings through history as the slayer of "separate but equal," filed a new suit against the Topeka school system—in 1979—claiming that her own children still suffered a segregated education. There had been a period of rapid school integration in the late 1960s and early 1970s, but the trend was reversed by the backlash against court-ordered busing to achieve racial balance in the schools. By the time the Supreme Court decided *Brown III* in Brown's favor, in 1984, public schools had been largely resegregated.

THE POLITICS OF RACE

The most enduring of the civil rights era's villains, Alabama's governor George Wallace, attracted a large following in the North as well as in the South by appealing to racial prejudice. He was making his third run for president in 1972 when a would-be assassin gunned him down campaigning in Maryland. Confined to a wheelchair, he was elected to a fourth term as Alabama's governor in 1982 on the strength of the black vote. (Considering that Wallace's political program always favored the have-nots, this may not be as strange as it at first seems.)

Wallace personally apologized to the old Movement champions, including Rosa Parks, Ralph Abernathy, and Coretta Scott King. In 1979, Wallace had coffee with John Lewis, who had been permanently scarred by the governor's men at Selma's Edmund Pettus Bridge, and said, "I want to ask your forgiveness." (Lewis's other colorful antagonist, Selma's sheriff Jim Clark, pleaded guilty in 1978 to charges of conspiring to smuggle marijuana.)

Wallace's "redemption" was in no small part due to the civil rights movement's rearrangement of the South's political geography: He needed the black vote. In local politics, African Americans are now elected to office in numbers that reflect their percentage of the population. On the national political scene, however, the Movement brought an unintended bonanza for the Republicans: Once the Democrats became identified with President John F. Kennedy's Civil Rights Act of 1964 and Lyndon B. Johnson's Voting Rights Act of 1965, they lost their white southern base. Today, the Republican Party of Lincoln—of Emancipation and Reconstruction—has become the party of the white Southerner.

THE FATE OF MARTIN LUTHER KING

It's interesting that the first federal holiday in honor of Martin Luther King was observed, in 1986, under Ronald Reagan, a president whose administration was unapologetically inattentive to black Americans. (In an appeal to white voters, Reagan had kicked off his 1980 campaign in Philadelphia, Mississippi, where Freedom Summer workers Schwerner, Chaney, and Goodman had been murdered in 1964.) Ironically, the annual observances of King's birthday every January have stripped him of much of his power to inspire and transform. His nonviolence is sold as passivity by those who want to discourage black folks from making demands on power.

The most popular line from the "I Have a Dream" speech is King's hope that his children "will not be judged by the color of their skin but by the content of their character," though those quoting it are often justifying their opposition to government programs designed to boost black employment and education opportunities. Fixed in that moment, at the March on Washington in 1963, King remains the eternal dreamer, and we sometimes lose sight of the tough solutions he proposed at the end of his life, calling for America to redistribute among all its citizens the sacrifices carried by its black people. There was still much unfinished work at the time of King's death in 1968.

MEANING

I heard the news of Martin Luther King's assassination on a car radio while on my way to Loveman's—one of the department stores his SCLC had gotten desegregated five years earlier—to have my picture taken for a portrait of my high school sorority, an "exclusive" club of the most privileged white girls in Birmingham, Alabama. I felt an intense stab of regret at the violent end of a human life. But I was still, at 15, enough of a child of segregation to think that King's death meant that all the South's problems would be over. Birmingham would return to the happy community it had been before the "troublemaker" came. And my father would no longer have to go out at night fighting the white South's anti–civil rights crusade, which had continued beyond the fall of segregation itself.

Part of what inspired me to write my first book, *Carry Me Home,* was my fear that my father might have been a member of the Ku Klux Klan, that he knew the men who had bombed Birmingham's Sixteenth Street Baptist Church, killing four black girls near my age. *Carry Me Home* began as a detective story about Papa's troubling role in our city's date with destiny. In the end, although I concluded that he had not been in the Klan, I never quite got to the bottom of what he was doing those nights when his "civil rights meetings" took him out after dark into the Magic City. But in the course of trying, I discovered how I fit into the world. Having a father who opposed the civil rights movement had ironically given me the passion to take up its cause, as a writer, 20 years later. Today Papa is a stranger to the fierce bigot he was in 1963, but he did not mind the blunt revelations I made about him in my book. After reading it he said, "I didn't realize my life had that much meaning."

That is why the story of the civil rights movement retains such a hold on our national imagination: It gives America meaning. The experience of African Americans keeps all Americans mindful of the worst we are capable of as a nation, the inhumanity we are willing to legislate and defend. But it also reveals the best of the human spirit, the potential for the advancement of civilization when an oppressed people raise us all up in the course of lifting up themselves. The slaves' descendants remind us that democracy is not a fact but an ideal, requiring us to strive constantly for more while taking nothing for granted.

Even if the Promised Land remains somewhere out there on the horizon, beyond the tricky roadblock of economic injustice, the civil rights movement put freedom on the map, and made it the destination for many people around the globe. The Movement is a model that showed others—women, the disabled, and non-heterosexuals—how to lay claim to the Declaration of Independence's unalienable right to the pursuit of happiness. In the world community, the United States' civil rights struggle inspired the democratic revolutions that overthrew Communism in Czechoslovakia and apartheid in South Africa.

I hope that the civil rights movement has also made you wonder how your life may be intersecting with the grand plan of the present era, what John Lewis calls "the spirit of history." Have no doubt: History is going on around you right now. You can either make it or it will make you. No one knows while it's happening how it will turn out. But everything counts.

SELECTED BIBLIOGRAPHY

In the 20 years that I have been studying the civil rights revolution, I interviewed many participants, sifted through numerous archives, and read countless books and articles that have gone into the writing of *A Dream of Freedom*. Below is a selective list of sources to which I am particularly indebted and which provided direct quotes used in this book.

Abernathy, Ralph David. *And the Walls Came Tumbling Down*. Harper & Row, 1989.

Branch, Taylor. *Parting the Waters: America in the King Years, 1954–63*. Simon & Schuster, 1988.

_____. *Pillar of Fire: America in the King Years 1963–65*. Simon & Schuster, 1998.

Beals, Melba Pattillo. *Warriors Don't Cry*. Pocket Books, 1994.

Broderick, Francis L., and August Meier, eds. *Negro Protest Thought in the Twentieth Century*. Bobbs-Merrill Company, 1965.

Cagin, Seth, and Philip Dray. *We Are Not Afraid: The Story of Goodman, Schwerner, and Chaney and the Civil Rights Campaign for Mississippi*. Macmillan, 1988.

Carson, Clayborne. *In Struggle: SNCC and the Black Awakening of the 1960s*. Harvard University Press, 1981.

Carter, Dan T. *The Politics of Rage: George Wallace, the Origins of the New Conservatism, and the Transformation of American Politics*. Simon & Schuster, 1995.

Clark, E. Culpepper. *The Schoolhouse Door: Segregation's Last Stand at the University of Alabama*. Oxford University Press, 1993.

Coles, Robert. *Children of Crisis: A Study of Courage and Fear*. Dell, 1967.

Doyle, William. *An American Insurrection: The Battle of Oxford, Mississippi, 1962*. Doubleday, 2001.

Dyson, Michael Eric. *I May Not Get There with You: The True Martin Luther King, Jr.* Touchstone Books, 2001.

Fairclough, Adam. *Better Day Coming: Blacks and Equality, 1890–2000*. Viking, 2001.

_____. *To Redeem the Soul of America: The Southern Christian Leadership Conference and Martin Luther King, Jr.* University of Georgia Press, 1987.

Fosl, Catherine. *Subversive Southerner: Anne Braden and the Struggle for Racial Justice in the Cold War South*. Palgrave Macmillan, 2002.

Garrow, David J. *Bearing the Cross: Martin Luther King, Jr., and the Southern Christian Leadership Conference*. Morrow, 1986.

Gates, Henry Louis, Jr., and Cornel West. *The African-American Century: How Black Americans Have Shaped Our Country*. Free Press, 2000.

Hampton, Henry, and Steve Fayer. *Voices of Freedom: An Oral History of the Civil Rights Movement from the 1950s through the 1980s*. Bantam, 1990.

Henderson, Cheryl Brown. "Brown v. Board of Education at Fifty: A Personal Perspective." *The College Board Review*, Fall 2003.

Hendrickson, Paul. *Sons of Mississippi: A Story of Race and Its Legacy*. Knopf, 2003.

Keiler, Allan. *Marian Anderson: A Singer's Journey*. Scribner, 2000.

Kennedy, Stetson. *Jim Crow Guide: The Way It Was*. 1959; Atlantic University Press, 1990.

King, Coretta Scott. *My Life with Martin Luther King, Jr.* Holt, Rinehart and Winston, 1969.

King, Martin Luther, Jr. *Why We Can't Wait*. New American Library, 1964.

Kluger, Richard. *Simple Justice: The History of Brown v. Board of Education and Black America's Struggle for Equality*. Knopf, 1976.

Leventhal, Willy S., ed. *The Children Coming on: A Retrospective of the Montgomery Bus Boycott*. River City Publishing, 1998.

Levine, Ellen. *Freedom's Children: Young Civil Rights Activists Tell Their Own Stories*. Avon, 1993.

Lewis, David Levering. *W.E.B. Du Bois: Biography of a Race, 1868–1919*. Holt, 1993.

Lewis, John, with Michael D'Orso. *Walking with the Wind: A Memoir of the Movement*. Simon & Schuster, 1998.

Loveland, Anne C. *Lillian Smith: A Southerner Confronting the South*. Louisiana State University Press, 1986.

McWhorter, Diane. *Carry Me Home: Birmingham, Alabama—The Climactic Battle of the Civil Rights Revolution*. Simon & Schuster, 2001.

Manchester, William. *The Glory and the Dream: A Narrative History of America, 1932–1972*. Little, Brown, 1974.

Martinez, Elizabeth, ed. *Letters from Mississippi*. Zephyr Press, 2002.

Navasky, Victor. *Kennedy Justice*. Atheneum, 1977.

Nossiter, Adam. *Of Long Memory: Mississippi and the Murder of Medgar Evers*. Perseus Publishing, 1994.

O'Reilly, Kenneth. *"Racial Matters": The FBI's Secret File on Black America, 1960–1972*. Free Press, 1989.

Packard, Jerrold M. *American Nightmare: The History of Jim Crow*. St. Martin's Press, 2002.

Raines, Howell. *My Soul Is Rested: Movement Days in the Deep South Remembered*. Penguin, 1983.

Till-Mobley, Mamie, and Christopher Benson. *Death of Innocence: The Story of the Hate Crime That Changed America*. Random House, 2003.

Viorst, Milton. *Fire in the Streets*. Simon & Schuster, 1979.

Wade, Wyn Craig. *The Fiery Cross: The Ku Klux Klan in America*. Simon & Schuster, 1987.

Williams, Juan. *Eyes on the Prize: America's Civil Rights Years, 1954–1965*. Viking, 1987.

FOR FURTHER READING

WEB SITES

The Afro-American Almanac (http://www.toptags.com/aama)

The Martin Luther King Jr. Papers Project at Stanford University
(http://www.stanford.edu/group/King)

AT&T Knowledge Network Explorer: Black History Homepage
(http://www.kn.att.com/wired/BHM/index.html)

BOOKS TO READ

Bolden, Tonya. *Tell All the Children Our Story: Memories and
Mementos of Being Young and Black*. Harry N. Abrams, 2002.

Bridges, Ruby. *Through My Eyes*. Scholastic, 1999.

King, Casey, and Linda Barrett Osborne. *Oh, Freedom! Kids Talk
About the Civil Rights Movement With the People Who Made It
Happen*. Knopf, 1997.

King, Martin Luther, Jr. *I Have a Dream*. Scholastic, 1997.

Meltzer, Milton. *There Comes a Time: The Struggle for Civil
Rights*. Random Library, 2001.

Rochelle, Belinda. *Witnesses to Freedom: Young People Who
Fought for Civil Rights*. Puffin, 1997

Smith, Lillian. *Killers of the Dream*. W.W. Norton, 1994.

Wormser, Richard. *The Rise and Fall of Jim Crow*. St. Martin's
Press, 2003.

INDEX

AFTER THE SPILL

The **Exxon Valdez** Disaster
Then and Now

Sandra Markle

WALKER AND COMPANY

More than 11 million gallons of gooey black oil poured into the sea— enough to fill about fourteen Olympic-sized swimming pools. The greasy oil that poured out of the Exxon Valdez floated to the surface, then washed ashore, coating 2,490 kilometers (1,548 miles) of shoreline. The gray areas in the picture on page 3 are oil-covered land.

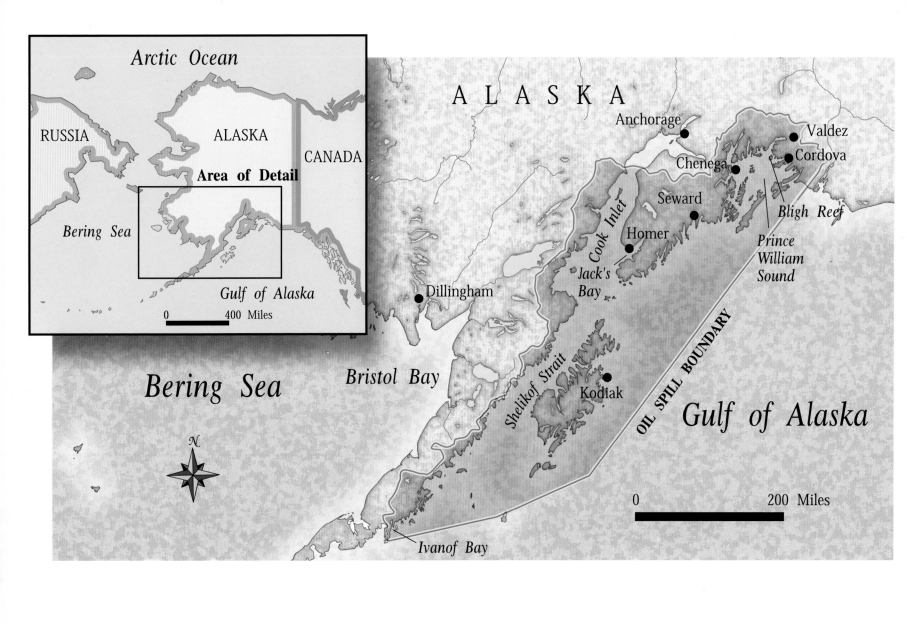

Arctic Ocean

RUSSIA

ALASKA

CANADA

Area of Detail

Bering Sea

Gulf of Alaska

0   400 Miles

ALASKA

Anchorage

Valdez

Chenega

Cordova

Seward

Cook Inlet

Homer

Bligh Reef

Jack's
Bay

Prince
William
Sound

Dillingham

Bering Sea

Bristol Bay

Shelikof Strait

Kodiak

OIL SPILL BOUNDARY

Gulf of Alaska

N

0   200 Miles

Ivanof Bay

What Happened Here?

Imagine the mess if you punched a can opener into the bottom of an aluminum can full of soda. Now, imagine ripping a hole in the bottom of a ship full of oil—a ship that's longer than three football fields and extends down into the water as far as an upside-down five-story building.

That's what happened just seconds after midnight on March 24, 1989. Crossing Prince William Sound to the Pacific Ocean, the crewman on duty spotted ice ahead and turned the *Exxon Valdez* out of the ship's normal route. Too big to turn easily, the ship went far off course and struck Bligh Reef, a jumble of jagged boulders just twelve meters (forty feet) below the water's surface. The rocks ripped open the ship's metal hull.

What happened next was a disaster. Cleaning up the mess cost several billion dollars and has taken years.

Why Was This Spill Such a Big Problem?

Aleyska, the company responsible for transporting the oil, was called within minutes of the wreck, but the spill took everyone by surprise. Nobody had thought such a big oil spill would ever happen, so Aleyska was caught unprepared. Although workers at Aleyska knew how to handle an ordinary spill, there weren't enough resources to clean up after the *Exxon Valdez*.

Besides being large, the *Exxon Valdez* spill was difficult to clean because of its remote location. The only way to reach the spill was by helicopter or boat.

Because the weather was clear and the sea was very calm, Aleyska officials thought the oil would just stay pooled around the shipwreck. For three days, the company's spill experts tested different plans to find the best way to clean up the spill. Then something unexpected happened. A fierce storm with high winds created strong waves that pushed the oil away from the wreck and onto the beaches. Now the mess was a disaster.

What Happened to the Animals?

This bird didn't expect oil to be floating on the water when it landed on the waves in search of a fish dinner. Its feathers immediately became coated with the oil, which let cold water reach the bird's skin. When the bird tried to clean its feathers by pulling them through its mouth, it was poisoned by swallowing the toxic oil. Many seabirds, such as cormorants and scoters, died from getting too cold or swallowing the oil.

Volunteers picked up and cleaned as many of the birds as they could, but it was a difficult process. An oily bird had to be dunked in warm soapy water while the feathers were scrubbed with a toothbrush to loosen the sticky oil. Then the soap had to be rinsed away. Usually the whole process needed to be repeated a second time. Sadly, this cleaning was stressful for the birds, and many of those that were rescued died in the process.

A bird's feathers are usually light and fluffy—perfect for trapping warm air next to the bird's skin. Coated with oil, the feathers make the bird as uncomfortable as you would be if you went outdoors to play in the snow in wet clothes.

Sea otters were victims of the *Exxon Valdez* oil spill too. When an otter swam into the oil or popped up through the slick to take a breath of air, it became coated with the sticky black stuff. Just like seabirds, sea otters depend on their fluffy coat to stay warm. Their fur traps air warmed by their body heat close to their skin. Matted with oil, the fur can no longer do its job. Naturally, the oil-coated otters tried to clean themselves the only way they knew how: by licking their fur. So they too were poisoned by swallowing the toxic oil.

Picking up oiled otters, cleaning them, and moving them to unoiled beaches took a lot of time, effort, and money. Experts at Exxon estimated that it cost about $80,000 each to rescue and clean the sea otters. Kathy Frost, of the Alaska Department of Fish and Game, reported that, sadly, many of the cleaned otters died anyway.

After they were cleaned up, sea otters were moved away from the spill area. Most of the cleaned sea otters were taken to Jack's Bay opposite Homer, Alaska, and set free.

According to the *Exxon Valdez* Oil Spill Trustee Council, the oil spill affected Alaska's pink salmon and sockeye salmon populations differently. Pink salmon leave the sea and swim up shallow streams to lay their eggs in the gravel. Waves pushed the oil up these streams, coating the pink salmon eggs. The oil killed the unborn baby salmon, greatly reducing the population of future pink salmon.

Unlike pink salmon, sockeye salmon swim way upstream and lay their eggs in lakes, so they were not affected by the spilled oil. However, since all salmon fishing was stopped the year after the spill, more adults than usual made it upstream to lay their eggs. The number of baby sockeye salmon that hatched was so large, their habitat became overcrowded. Many young sockeye salmon died because there was not enough food to feed all the hungry fish.

Pink salmon spawning at Prince William Sound.

11

The herring population suffered too. Because herring eggs float at the water's surface, they were coated by the oil. The year of the spill, the number of herring that hatched was much lower than normal.

Problems with the fish populations after the spill meant problems for the seabirds and sea otters that eat the fish. People were hurt too—especially those who depend on the herring fishing industry. Three years after the spill, the number of adult herring dropped so low it became hard for people to catch enough to make a living. Also, the fish that hatched during the spill had open sores, so they could not be sold for food.

To help the herring population recover, fishing was banned for a year and limited for several more years by the Alaska Department of Fish and Game. That strategy worked for the fish, but it was hard for people who depended on fishing for their living. Some could not afford to keep their fishing boats. A number of people who worked in fish processing plants moved away and took other jobs.

Weakened by the oil spill, much of the herring population suffered from a virus that attacks weak fish. The virus causes open sores like the ones on the affected fish at the top of the photograph.

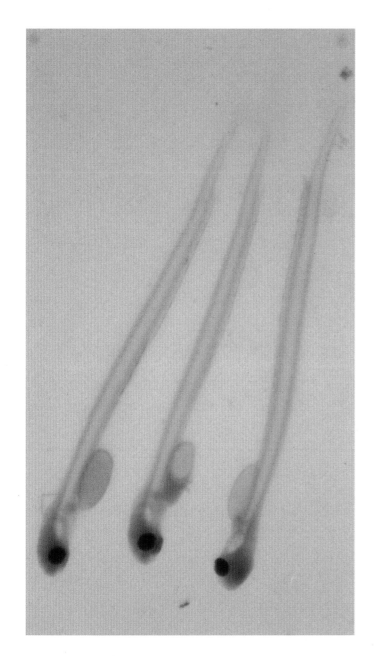

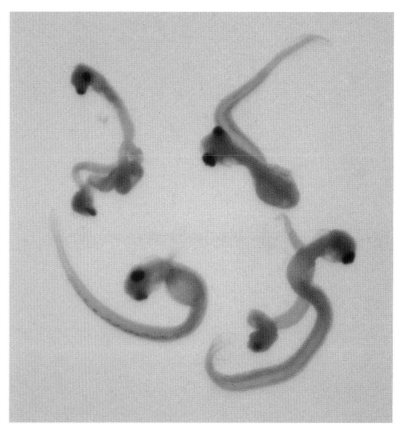

Many of the herring that hatched in the oil-polluted water were deformed. These photographs show healthy, normal herring (left) and deformed herring larvae (above).

Did the Oil Spill Affect People Too?

One place especially affected by the oil spill was Chenega, a small village on the edge of Prince William Sound.

The residents of Chenega are mainly Native Americans who, like their grandparents and great-grandparents, have always depended on Prince William Sound for food. Living much the way their ancestors did, the Chenega residents collected mussels on the beach and caught fish and seals.

When the black oil sloshed ashore on Chenega's beach, this community changed forever.

This is a view of Chenega. This wasn't the first time Chenega faced disaster. In 1964 an earthquake destroyed the village and residents had to rebuild.

14

After the spill, the people of Chenega were afraid to eat anything that came from the Sound. Scientists reported that any fish or seals that survived the spill were safe to eat, but the people of Chenega did not believe the reports. Without the natural resources of the Sound, Chenega residents were forced to take drastic action to feed their families.

Many left Chenega to find jobs. They worked on the oil cleanup teams or in the town of Valdez. With the money they earned, they bought food and hired a plane to fly the supplies to Chenega. Later, when the crisis was over, some people decided they liked living in a more modern town. Because they never returned, the population of Chenega is now only about half the size it was before the spill.

A boom, a floating fence, was supposed to trap oil washed off the Chenega shore so it could be skimmed up. However, tides repeatedly pushed under the fence and washed the oil back onto the shore before it could be collected. Then the beach had to be sprayed clean again.

The spill also changed Valdez, even though it was not directly affected by the oil. Because the town was the center of the cleanup operation, its population exploded within weeks after the spill, going from 3,500 to over 13,000 people. Imagine having the population of your town grow to more than three times its size in just a few weeks!

Most of the new people in town were cleanup workers. There were also Exxon officials, scientists, volunteers to help the animals, and newspaper and television reporters from around the world. The few hotels in town were quickly filled. Soon every family with an empty bedroom was renting to a stranger, and vacant lots were filled with tents.

Before the spill, most of the boats in this harbor would have been fishing boats. During the cleanup, every available boat in the harbor was hired by Exxon. Now many are tour boats.

The Keystone Hotel (inset) has a special connection to the spill. It was originally built by Exxon and served as its headquarters during the cleanup operation (shown above). After the cleanup, bathrooms were added to the offices to transform the building into a hotel.

Just after the spill, cars and boats were even harder to find than beds. There were no rental cars in town, so for a while, some families earned extra money by renting their cars. Later, to fill the huge demand, cars arrived by the truckload.

It was a boost to the economy to have so many people in Valdez, but it was also hard for such a small town to support so many people. Trucks loaded with food had to be hauled into town to feed everyone. There were also increased demands for basic services such as electricity, water, and sewage treatment.

19

The cleanup lasted a very long time—mainly from 1989 through 1992. In some places, the cleanup effort is still going on. In others, the beaches are back to normal.

What Is Being Done to Prevent Future Spills?

In the event of a future oil spill, the crew of a SERVS vessel would start cleanup immediately. In case of a leak while a tanker is being filled, a containment boom surrounds the ship (bottom left).

As a result of the *Exxon Valdez* oil spill, Congress passed the Oil Pollution Act in 1990 to help prevent future accidents. Today, oil tankers are stronger, and there are more safeguards against spills.

The SERVS (Ship Escort & Response Vessel Service) vessel is especially equipped to handle cleanup operations. Under what looks like two orange domes (right) on the rear deck are big hoses designed to suck oil off the surface of the water.

SERVS also maintains cleanup barges at several locations in the Sound. Because precious time could be wasted transporting crews to remote locations in the Sound, workers take turns waiting close to places where ships could get into trouble and possibly cause an oil spill.

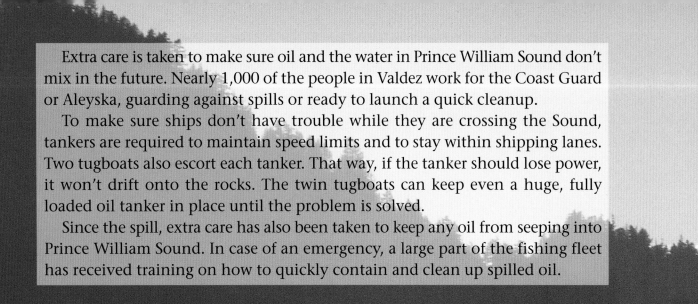

Extra care is taken to make sure oil and the water in Prince William Sound don't mix in the future. Nearly 1,000 of the people in Valdez work for the Coast Guard or Aleyska, guarding against spills or ready to launch a quick cleanup.

To make sure ships don't have trouble while they are crossing the Sound, tankers are required to maintain speed limits and to stay within shipping lanes. Two tugboats also escort each tanker. That way, if the tanker should lose power, it won't drift onto the rocks. The twin tugboats can keep even a huge, fully loaded oil tanker in place until the problem is solved.

Since the spill, extra care has also been taken to keep any oil from seeping into Prince William Sound. In case of an emergency, a large part of the fishing fleet has received training on how to quickly contain and clean up spilled oil.

To make sure every tanker stays safely away from Bligh Reef where the Exxon Valdez *ran aground, the rocks are now marked with a lighted beacon. Buoys define the sea lane.*

What Is Prince William Sound Like Today?

The oil spill also changed Valdez by making it world famous. Tourists flock to the area every summer to see this special place they discovered on the news. Before the spill, Valdez only had 20 bed-and-breakfasts. During the cleanup operation, that number exploded to 150, and today there are still about 100—proof of a strong tourist business.

Large areas of land and portions of the Sound have been closed to commercial fishing and land development. Protecting these areas helps animal populations recover. At the same time, it also serves as a way to attract tourists. An abundance of campsites, trails, and docks enable people to enjoy this beautiful area.

In the summer, it's daylight in Valdez nearly twenty-four hours a day, so tourists have plenty of time to enjoy the area's many activities.

23

How Are the Animals Today?

What about the animals that live in or around Prince William Sound? Have they recovered from the oil spill? The answer depends on the kind of animal.

It's uncertain whether the sea otter population will recover from the spill, but success depends in part on the recovery of their habitat. For sea otters to do well, the populations of the fish, crabs, and snails that they eat must recover too. The key is the recovery of brown seaweed in the area just offshore. The large leaves of the adult plants are home to snails and limpets and shelter young fish. Besides being oiled, the brown seaweed was killed by the high-pressure, hot-water wash used to clean the beaches. This just goes to show that anything that disrupts an environment hurts the whole web of life living there.

The sea otter's survival is tied to the recovery of brown seaweed, which houses the snails and crabs that the otters eat.

The bald eagle population was the first to rebound. The year after the spill, it was already on the rise. By 1997, it was the only population to be listed as fully recovered by the *Exxon Valdez* Oil Spill Trustee Council. After the spill, bald eagles that had been unable to find suitable nests took over the nests abandoned by birds that had died. The most recent survey taken in 1997 counted about 5,000 bald eagles living around the Sound—1,000 more than before the spill.

Prince William Sound is once again a good place for eagles to fish.

The oil spill hurt some animals that were already in trouble. For example, the harbor seal population was already low. Then hundreds of seals died because of the spill. Rather than recovering, the seal population has continued to shrink. Researchers are trying to understand why this decline is occurring. Because harbor seals travel long distances to hunt for fish, researchers are using monitoring devices and satellites to track the seals and may soon know exactly where they go to find food.

Other animal populations, including cormorants and pigeon guillemots, have also decreased. No one is quite sure why this is the case or if these animal populations will rebound in the future. Everyone knows for sure that future oil spills must be prevented if these animals are to survive.

Many harbor seal pups died after being born on oily beaches.

Is the Oily Mess Completely Cleaned Up?

What about the community of Chenega? It's still struggling to recover. Even the effort to clean up its beach continues. So much oil washed ashore that despite repeated cleanup efforts, oil continues to seep out of the sand beneath the rocks.

It may take many more years, but eventually the weather and the waves will clean away all traces of the *Exxon Valdez* oil spill from the beaches of Prince William Sound—even from Chenega. The emotional impact of the spill, though, can't be corrected by the forces of nature. Those changes are likely to have an effect—for better or worse—that lasts forever.

Larry Evanoff sits on the beach at Chenega in the summer of 1997—eight years after the spill. He is holding a tarry ball of weathered oil that was just removed from the beach.

Glossary/Index

Aleyska: The company that runs the Trans-Alaska Pipeline and loads the oil into tankers in Port Valdez. From there, the oil is transported to refineries. 5, 19

Animal Cleaning: Volunteers worked together to clean up oiled animals—a process that was very stressful for the animals. 6–9

Bald Eagle: This predatory bird has a large head, a short tail, and a wing span as great as 200 centimeters (80 inches). Young eagles have brown heads until they are about four years old. Mature adults have white heads. 24–25

Bligh Reef: A jumble of rocks that makes the Sound shallow—too shallow for a big tanker to cross safely. 4, 18

Chenega: A small village on an island in Prince William Sound that relies on fishing and seal hunting to support its economy. During the 1964 Alaska earthquake, the town was badly damaged and had to be rebuilt. 14–17, 28, 29

Containment Boom: A floating barrier used to trap oil on the surface of the water. 16, 19

Exxon: A large oil company that owns the *Exxon Valdez* and many other oil tankers. 5, 9, 19

Exxon Valdez: The oil supertanker that caused the spill. After the spill, it was repaired but banned from Port Valdez. Renamed the *SeaRiver Mediterranean*, the ship continues to transport oil through the Mediterranean and up to northern Europe. 2–4, 21

Harbor Seal: A small marine mammal. Both males and females may grow to be as long as 2 meters (about 6 feet) and weigh over 136 kilograms (300 pounds). Their coloring varies from silver to black, but the most common is light gray with dark spots. 26–27

Herring: A large cold-water fish that is blue-green on top and silver along its sides. Herring are covered with large scales and may grow up to 45 centimeters (18 inches) in length. 12–13

Oil Slick: A layer of oil on the surface of the water. 4

Pigeon Guillemot: A small black bird with white markings on its wings. It eats fish in shallow waters near the shoreline of the Sound. 6, 7

Pink Salmon: One of the many breeds of salmon, the pink salmon is a blue-hued fish with pink flesh. It can grow up to 62 centimeters (about 25 inches) in length. Just before spawning, males turn black with white bellies and females become olive green with lighter green bellies. 10–11

Prince William Sound: An inlet of the Gulf of Alaska. Many animals use the Sound as a nursery for their young. 3–5, 18–19, 22–23, 28–29

Sea Otter: A furry marine mammal that is at home in the cold Alaskan water. It lacks a layer of fat to insulate it from the cold water, but has thick fur to keep it warm. 8–9, 22–23

Sockeye Salmon: This grayish silver fish changes to a deep red when it is ready to reproduce. The adults grow to be over 50 centimeters (20 inches) long and weigh as much as 3 kilograms (about 6 pounds). 11

SERVS: This is the Ship Escort & Response Vessel Service. It is charged with the job of preventing future oil spills in Prince William Sound and Valdez. 18

Valdez: A town that serves as both a fishing harbor and the shipping point for oil from Alaska. 18–19

For the children of Chenega.

The author thanks the following individuals for sharing their enthusiasm and expertise: Dr. Alan Mearns, leader, BioAssessment team, Hazardous Materials Response and Assessment Division, NOAA; Deborah Payton, oceanographer, Modeling and Simulation Studies team of NOAA/ HAZMAT; John Wilcock, fishery research biologist, Alaska Department of Fish and Game; and Dr. Kathy Frost, biologist, Alaska Department of Fish and Game.

First published in the United States of America in 1999 by Walker Publishing Company, Inc.

Published simultaneously in Canada by Fitzhenry and Whiteside, Markham, Ontario L3R 4T8

Library of Congress Cataloging-in-Publication Data
Markle, Sandra.
After the spill: the *Exxon Valdez* disaster, then and now/Sandra Markle.
p. cm.
Summary: Examines the impact of the 1989 *Exxon Valdez* oil spill on the environment and people of Prince William Sound and describes the steps taken to minimize the damage and prevent a recurrence.
ISBN 0–8027–8610–3 (hc.) —ISBN 0–8027–8611–1 (rein.)
1. Oil spills—Environmental aspects—Alaska—Prince William Sound Region—Juvenile literature. 2. Tankers—Accidents—Environmental aspects—Alaska—Prince William Sound Region—Juvenile literature. 3. *Exxon Valdez* (Ship)—Juvenile literature. [1. Oil spills—Alaska—Prince William Sound Region. 2. Tankers—Accidents. 3. *Exxon Valdez* (Ship)] I. Title.
TD427.P4M377 1999
363.738'2'097983—dc21

98–38550
CIP
AC

Photo Credits: Larry Evanoff: 14; Exxon: 19, 20; Kathy Frost: 28; Greenpeace: 6; Rich Kirchner: 8, 10, 24, 26; Jim Lavrakas, *Anchorage Daily News*: 29; Sandra Markle: 1, 16, 18, 19, 21, 22, 23, 31; Oil Spill Public Information Center: 16; Chris Rose, U. S. Coast Guard: 2, 3; John Wilcock, Alaska Department of Fish and Game: 12, 13.

Map on page 4 © Joe LeMonnier

The front jacket photograph, by Kathy Frost, was taken two months after the spill; the title page photograph (also on page 22), by Sandra Markle, depicts the area after the completion of the cleanup.

Book design by Maura Fadden Rosenthal/Mspace

Printed in Hong Kong

10 9 8 7 6 5 4 3 2 1